GOD'S PROMISES TO PREACHERS

Aaron Isaiah Jones

341
BROADMAN PRESS
Nashville, Tennessee

© Copyright 1982 • Broadman Press.

All rights reserved.

4222-40

ISBN: 0-8054-2240-4

Dewey Decimal Classification: 253

Subject heading: MINISTERS—SERMONS

Library of Congress Catalog Card Number: 81-67128

Printed in the United States of America

Dedication

To Pearl River Valley Baptist Church, which has encouraged and warmly supported my preaching ministry with prayers, pride, and provisions for a number of pleasant years. The profound faithfulness of this flock served to strengthen and sustain me during the preparation of these messages.

To my beloved and faithful wife, Mary Jane Crum Jones, who has been by my side down through the years and has gently and patiently prodded me to persevere during the penning of these sermons.

Acknowledgment

I wish to express my appreciation and gratitude to:

Mr. Edgar D. Bridges, the good and faithful chairman of our deacons' board, for his wonderful assistance in getting these messages typed and readied to be sent to my editor.

Dr. William P. Davis, president emeritus of Mississippi Baptist Seminary, for his fatherly advice and his liason work between this humble author and my editor and for his willingness to assist me in so many ways.

Preface

My life has been touched by ministers of the gospel of Jesus Christ for as long as I can remember. As a tiny tot, I had the unique experience of living in a pastor's parsonage. I can still remember and see my father, the Reverend Lee Jones, coming in from his church with his familiar Bible in his hand or carrying his black briefcase with his preaching paraphernalia within. My father was a dynamic Bible preacher who electrified people with his vivid and graphic interpretive preaching. He inspired me very early in my life by the power of his preaching and by the Christian life that he lived before people.

Reverend C. L. (Sin-Killing) Lindsey who pastored a little Baptist Church on "Nixon Hill" in Biloxi, Mississippi, also inspired me during my childhood days. My brother Enoch and I would often attend the old-fashioned tent meetings held in our hometown of Gulfport, Mississippi, where Brother Lindsey preached. The Lord blessed Brother Lindsey with a long and fruitful life as a pastor and an evangelist. After Enoch and I had completed our service in the armed forces during World War II, and were honorably discharged, we'd often ride the bus from Gulfport to Biloxi on Sunday afternoons to hear Brother Lindsey preach. The memory of the minister's messages still lingers in my heart.

Reverend J. J. McQueen, Jr., of Alabama, who preached to me at Mount Bethel Baptist Church at Gulfport, was the next minister who inspired me greatly by his ministry. He took time out from a busy schedule to teach us to sing songs of Zion, and he helped us to develop our athletic skills on the baseball and the softball diamonds along the Mississippi Gulf coast. More than once, this kind preaching man took us, by way of a chartered bus, to cities in both Mississippi and Alabama, to perform musical programs. We would rejoice in the rich, unforgettable experience of fellowshipping with other young Christians in our own age bracket. During these programs, Brother McQueen would sing and preach as an enrichment to our programs. This great man of God inspired me and many other young Christians in a little town where it was very difficult for young people to live a constant Christian life.

The Reverend Dr. T. B. Brown, who pastored Enoch and me after the

World War II years, at Mount Bethel Baptist Church, perhaps inspired me most when I was struggling with answering the call to the gospel ministry of Jesus Christ. What a marvelous role he played in my life at a most crucial point! Under his wise pastoral counseling and his fatherly understanding, I answered the call of God. It was this wonderful shepherd who licensed me after I'd preached my "trial sermon." It was he who gave me my first Bible after I'd preached my first sermon. It was he who gave me my first donation toward my college and seminary training. And, thanks be to God, it was he who sent me off to the Bible College of American Baptist Theological Seminary at Nashville, Tennessee.

The Reverend Dr. Enoch Jones, my own brother, who pastored me during my student days in Nashville, Tennessee, inspired me to study diligently and to major in preaching. It was he who taught me how to spend long hours in prayer and preparation. It was he who encouraged me to hold onto God's unchanging hand, to keep the faith, and to persevere when the way seemed dark. And it was he who bade me to become a preaching preacher.

This humble servant would be remiss in gratitude and derelict in duty were I not to include the late great Dr. Sandy F. Ray (author of *Journeying Through a Jungle* by Broadman) as a minister of the gospel of Jesus Christ who greatly inspired me to greater heights as a preacher. This man truly was a peerless preacher. He was a preaching preacher who was indeed a preacher's preacher. He inspired preachers. During the remainder of my preaching ministry, if the Christ of God would grant me one wish, it would be for the "mantle" of Sandy F. Ray to fall upon this humble preacher.

It is with profound gratitude to my God and King for his unspeakable gift of these ministers in my life that I prepare these messages for my fellow ministers, first here in Mississippi, and then for fellow ministers all over the world. If any of these humble messages can be used by any of the brethren anywhere, they have my blessings and my prayers.

In my preaching I often put the Scripture in my own words. I have found it a help to the congregation. These are not exact quotations from any translation. Any Scripture reference that is marked AT is my own. Unless marked otherwise, I have used the King James Version of the Bible. There are also times when a few words of a hymn will find their way into my sermon. They may be just a phrase that unconsciously finds its way into what I am saying. That is the way I preach. It would be cumbersome to footnote each use.

It is my prayer that preachers will find preaching material of their own from reading this book.

Contents

1

God's Promise
to a Preaching Preacher

Matthew 3:1-2;
Matthew 10:7

"In those days." The first three words in the first text suggest immediately that great mystery, intrigue, and suspenseful drama will be unfolded. "In those days"—three simple words consisting of only eleven letters in the alphabet. But, oh, the significance of those words. "In those days." These words seemingly leap out of the Bible and pounce upon a person. They suddenly grasp the attention of the hearer, capture the mind, and grip the imagination.

Yes, the first three words in the first text do at once let us know, suggestively so, that there was something strange, dramatic, and even frightening happening during the time of John the Baptist. "In those days." That they might sink and soak into your heart, mind, and soul, hear them again: "In those days." These three words prompt us to pose an all-important question: What manner of mystery and intrigue happening induced the saintly scribe to write, saying, "In those days"?

The saintly scribe referred to that particular time in this manner because "in those days" of which he writes, wrong and wickedness seemingly held a "winning hand" over righteousness. It seemed that truth was forever crushed to the ground while wrong had a perpetual seat on the throne. It seemed as if God had reneged on his covenant with Abraham, Isaac, and Jacob and had forgotten his promise to his people.

The Old Testament prophets had preached the promise of the coming of a Strong Deliverer. But now heaven seemed silent. Noah had preached 120 years, and his congregation had closed its ears to him. But, in the end, his God-inspired preaching plus his obedience to God saved himself and his family. Here, then, is a blessed lesson for all obedient, preaching preachers to learn. If any preacher can so preach and save himself and his family, that preacher has done himself some kind of preaching! Noah preached, and God saved him and his family.

Enoch walked with God. He walked right, and he talked right. Preachers of the gospel of Jesus Christ ought to walk right and talk right. Jesus Christ, the Bishop of our souls, says, "Let your communication be, Yea, yea; Nay, nay" (Matt. 5:37). Enoch had a righteous rap as he walked on with God. And one day they looked around, and Enoch was gone. God took him. "And Enoch walked with God: and he was not, for God took him" (Gen. 5:24).

Amos preached for justice to roll down as waters and righteousness as a mighty stream. Joel preached the promise of visions and dreams. Habakkuk cried, "O Lord, how long" (1:2). Obadiah preached and then slept with his fathers. Jonah, the reluctant prophet, finally went to Nineveh, and God knows that preacher preached. Micah preached powerfully and then slept, as did the prophets before him. Hosea preached with a broken heart while displaying a Godlike love for a bad wife and a stiff-necked people. He, too, had to move on from these murmuring shores.

Jeremiah saw a hammer (Jer. 23:29b). Ezekiel saw a wheel in the middle of a wheel (Ezek. 10:10). Daniel saw a stone (Dan. 2:34-35). Isaiah saw one coming from Edom with dyed garments from Bozrah (Isa. 63:1f.), treading the winepress alone and traveling in the greatness of his own strength.

Nahum preached about a devil who dashed people in pieces! Haggai preached that God's house should be built. Zephaniah, the son of Cushi, preached about a God who would gather up his children and make a name for them. Zechariah preached about a day that would come, with bells upon horses, reading, "Holiness unto the Lord."

Finally, Malachi, the last Old Testament preacher, preached his last sermon and closed his weeping, weary eyes in death. With the death of Malachi, an old dispensation was buried with him. For the next 430 years, (according to Old Testament scholars), no preaching prophet was heard in all Judea.

You know, that's a long time for people to live in a preachingless society. Four hundred and thirty years is a long time for families to fare without hearing from heaven by way of a preacher. Four hundred and thirty years is a long time for the head of a house to provide for his household without hearing the gospel of peace. Four hundred and thirty years is indeed a long, long time for a nation to endure without hearing the preacher say, "Blessed is the nation whose God is the Lord" (Ps. 33:12).

Yes, 430 years had passed since Malachi had gone off the scene. And well could the holy historian write: "In those days came John the Baptist, preaching in the wilderness of Judea, And saying, Repent ye: for the kingdom of heaven is at hand" (Matt. 3:1-2).

Repentance was the theme of John's message. The prophet called people to turn away from wickedness to behold the Lamb of God which taketh away the sins of the world. This wilderness prophet admonished those people who walked in darkness to behold One who would show them the marvelous light. He implored the sons of men to look unto the Son of God. At the heart of John's message was a fervent plea to the people to flee from the wrath to come.

In those days, wickedness had ascended the throne and sat snugly thereon with the black scepter of godlessness as the rule of the day. In those days, the Roman eagle spread its infamous wings all over the land of Palestine—from Dan to Beersheba. In those days, the glittering Caesar proudly proclaimed himself to be the divine ruler of the nations, and all roads led to Rome. In those days, John the Baptist came preaching, saying, "Repent ye: for the kingdom of heaven is at hand." The prophet warned them to flee from the wrath to come. He called them to repent and bear the fruit of righteousness for the kingdom of heaven. He announced to them that the axe was now laid at the root of the tree; therefore, every tree which bringeth not forth good fruit would be cut down and cast into the fire. This wilderness prophet preached to avert the wrath of God being poured out upon the people.

The city crowd which came into the country to hear this wilderness preacher wanted to know of him: "Just who are you anyhow? Are you the Promised One?" (See John 1:19f.) John's answer was sharp but simple enough. "You must not be able to read. For I am he of whom the prophet Isaiah wrote, 'The voice of one crying in the wilderness, Prepare ye the way of the Lord, make his paths straight. . . . I indeed baptize you with water unto repentance: but he that cometh after me is mightier than I, whose shoes I am not worthy to bear: he shall baptize you with the Holy Ghost, and with fire. Whose fan is in his hand: and he will thoroughly purge his floor, and gather his wheat into the garner; but he will burn up the chaff with unquenchable fire' " (see Matt. 3:3,11).

As John preached in those days when men turned away from sin and destruction to the Lord, and to light and to life, so must we preach in these days. We must preach in these days of silent shops, inactive assembly lines, high-rise projects, and sky-high living costs. In these days when the rich get richer and the poor get poorer, we must preach the gospel of reconciliation. You good shepherds of the flocks of God, be good and kind and compassionate to the people of God. Be counselors and community builders. By the divine authority of the big Book, I admonish you to do your duty with a shepherd's heart full of love. Visit the sick and the shut-ins. Pray for the distressed and the downtrodden. Seek out those who've gone astray. Lift up the fallen, bind up the brokenhearted, and give the sheep beauty for the soggy, gray ashes of their disappointments and their defeats. But while doing all of these things and many other pastoral duties, don't neglect your preaching. Feed the flock of God over which the Holy Ghost hath made you the overseer.

The God of our salvation, the Captain of our faith, the Bishop of our souls, and the Lord of our lives says, "As ye go, preach, saying, The kingdom of heaven is at hand" (Matt. 10:7).

May God bless all of those good churches all over this world who stand by their shepherds in every loving way. By virtue of divine authority as a minister of the gospel of Jesus Christ, I send to you my preacher's peace and my God-given love. Take this peace and love and spread it all over your church, community, and city. Churches, pray for your shepherd. And, brother deacons, stand around your shepherd and hold up his arms and be his armor bearers as he preaches the gospel of Jesus Christ.

And good wives, stand by your preaching husbands. Be patient and kind. Pray for them and pray with them. Be tenderhearted helpmates. Be sympathetic listeners. Be kind, compassionate friends. God has a great reward laid up in store for all of you good, kind, tenderhearted, compassionate, loving preachers' wives.

As you go, my preaching brethren, preach, saying, "The kingdom of heaven is at hand." Be preaching preachers. You have a mandate from the Master to go and to preach. A divine necessity has been laid upon you. He who laid this burden (preaching) upon you has also promised to keep a divine vigil over you.

Never before in the history of mankind has the need for God-sent, preaching preachers, been so keenly felt. We see crime in the streets of our cities. There's corruption in many of our state governments. Pimps, prostitutes, punks, and pushers brazenly walk our city streets and sidewalks within the shadows of our police precincts, seemingly unmolested and unafraid. We have big problems with corruption and immorality even in our small cities. The preacher must preach. Duty demands it. The land in which we live and love is hurting for the voice of a preaching preacher. The whole wide world is calling out to every preaching preacher, saying, "Is there any word from the Lord?" (Jer. 37:17).

The prophets of the Lord must be able to read the signs of the time by God's sundial. They must address themselves to the issues now at hand with what thus saith the Lord. The big Book calls to preachers of the gospel of Jesus Christ all over this world today, saying, "Watchmen, what of the night?" (Isa. 21:12, AT). The world is waiting for an answer. People all over the world need to hear preaching preachers. For "how shall they hear without a preacher? And how shall they preach, except they be sent?" (Rom. 10:14-15).

Brother preachers, preach the Word as never before. This is indeed your hour. Preach until the prodigal sons come home. Preach until wayward daughters fall out with the ways of the world and return to the fold of faith. Preach until every valley shall be exalted, every mountain made low, and the crooked be made straight. Preach until the Spirit of the Lord comes from the four winds and is poured out, and all flesh shall see it together.

But don't stop there. Preach until your sons and your daughters shall prophesy, and your young men shall see visions, and your old men shall dream dreams. Preach until the lost shall come saying, "Men and brethren, what shall we do to be saved?" (Compare Acts 16:30.)

But don't even stop there. Preach until justice rolls down as water and righteousness as a mighty stream. Preach until the knowledge of the Lord shall cover the earth as the waters cover the sea.

Maybe you feel that, like Peter of old, you've fished faithfully all the night season and have taken nothing. Well, by faith, go back, as he did, and try again. Don't ever tire of going back to let down the gospel net again and again. As you go, remember the eternal Christ is by your side. He keeps an eternal vigil upon the seashore of life. He is the eternal keeper of the lighthouse along the shores of life. He is with you. He bids you now, as he bade Peter then, to go back and try again. Every God-called, God-loving, God-fearing preaching preacher must, like Peter, be willing to say, "Nevertheless, by thy word," (Luke 5:5) and go back and try again. Keep on going back—keep on trying. There is an eternal Friend with you now. He'll be with you still, at the end of your quest.

He Understands, He'll Say "Well Done"

If when you give the best of your service,
Telling the world that the Savior is come;

Be not dismayed when men don't believe you;
He understands; He'll say, "Well done."

Misunderstood, the Savior of sinners,
Hung on the cross; He was God's only Son;
Oh! hear Him calling His Father in Heav'n,
"Not my will, but Thine be done."

If when this life of labor is ended,
And the reward of the race you have run;
Oh! the sweet rest prepared for the faithful,
Will be His blest and final "well done."

But if you try and fail in your trying,
Hands sore and scarred from the work you've begun;
Take up your cross, run quickly to meet him;
He'll understand; He'll say, "Well done."

Oh, when I come to the end of my journey,
Weary of life and the battle is won;
Carr'ing the staff and cross of redemption,
He'll understand, and say, "Well done."

Lucie E. Campbell

2

God's Grace
for an Afflicted Preacher

2 Corinthians 12:7-9

In this passage, the apostle shares with us the eternal safety and security found in the grace of God. Paul had had an out-of-this-world experience with God. Apparently it had afflicted him, temporarily, with a "Little Jack Horner" attitude toward himself. You remember the Mother Goose rhyme of yesteryear. It went like this: "Little Jack Horner/ Sat in a corner/ Eating his Christmas pie./ He stuck in his thumb/ And pulled out a plum/ And said, "What a good boy am I." Of course, we know it didn't take very much effort to break a thin pie crust. Nor did pulling out a plum make a good boy of a tiny tot.

The apostle relates to us in the first part of the textual chapter how he was caught up into the third heaven. He was caught up, as it were, into paradise, and heard unspeakable words which it is not lawful for a man to utter. Paul is careful to tell us that, "Of such an one will I glory: yet of myself I will not glory, but in mine infirmities" (2 Cor. 12:5).

Here was a preaching preacher who was willing to forego glorying in an out-of-this-world experience and rather glory in his infirmities. How often has this humble preacher reminded himself, after a "Pentecostal Sunday," not to glory in the sermon but rather in the Power and Source of the sermon.

Full many a time preachers are tempted to stand in the market-places on Monday and relate to the passerby how "they set them running on the Lord's Day." Many ministers are seemingly so fired up from Sunday that on Monday they are moved to take tape recordings of their message to a Monday congregation for approval.

It is my advice, after more than a quarter century of preaching the gospel of Jesus Christ, to use Monday to start the next Sunday's sermon. It is far better to use Monday making ready for the next Lord's Day than boasting in the marketplaces or playing taped sermons to Monday morning proof hearers.

Preaching the gospel of Jesus Christ is serious business. It is a matter of life or death. Paul knew this and thus cried out, "Woe is unto me, if I preach not the gospel!" (1 Cor. 9:16). Again, this great preaching preacher declared, "For I am not ashamed of the gospel of Christ: for it is the power of God unto salvation to everyone that believeth" (Rom. 1:16). The flock of God must be fed. It is a mandate from the Master. Monday morning is a marvelous time to begin preparing for this mandate.

The temptation to glory in our Sunday out-of-this-world experience on Monday is very great, but the feeding of the flock of God far outweighs the need to boast. Pastoring for twenty-five years has taught me that building sermons is better than boasting. Monday is a far better time to start than on Saturday. Saturday is too close to Sunday. Every preaching preacher ought to start getting ready for the next Sunday's sermon on Monday. A week isn't too long to prepare to preach. Sometimes it seems far too short. Preaching is a teasing, tantalizing task. Yes, it is serious business, a matter of life or death.

Paul knew the seriousness of preaching. This made the minister humble. It kept him meek and earnest. "For though I would desire to glory, I shall not be a fool; for I will say the truth: but now I forebear, lest any man should think of me above that which he seeth me to be, or that he heareth of me" (2 Cor. 12:6).

The apostle chose to be a fool for Christ rather than a fool for boasting. This, he found, was more profitable. His personal experience with Jesus Christ had taught him that glorying in an out-of-this-world experience was far less profitable than glorying in his affliction. He refused to take God's glory. He gave God the glory. "Of such a one will I glory: yet of myself I will not glory, but in mine infirmities" (2 Cor. 12:5).

Behold this preaching preacher! See his amazing courage! Lay hold upon his fruitful faith! Ever bear in mind the immortal words he writes, "Now faith is the substance of things hoped for, the evidence of things not seen. For by it the elders obtained a good report" (Heb. 11:1-2). Every preaching preacher ought to strive mightily to lay hold on this Paul-kind-of faith. Paul, near the end of his honor-roll-of-faith chapter concludes, for the benefit of preaching preachers everywhere:

> And what shall I more say? For the time would fail me to tell of Gedeon, and of Barak, and of Sampson, and Jephthae; of David also and Samuel, and of the prophets: Who through faith subdued kingdoms, wrought righteousness, obtained promises, stopped the mouths of lions, Quenched the violence of fire, escaped the edge of the sword, out of weakness were made strong, waxed valiant in fight, turned to flight the armies of the aliens. Women received their dead raised to life again; and others were tortured, not accepting deliverance; that they might obtain a better resurrection: And others had trial of cruel mockings and scourgings, yea, moreover of bonds and imprisonment: They were stoned, they were sawn asunder, were tempted, were slain with the sword: they wandered about in sheepskins and goatskins; being destitute, afflicted, tormented; (Of whom the world was not worthy:) they wandered in deserts, and in mountains, and in dens and caves of the earth. And these all, having obtained a good report through faith, received not the promise: God having provided some better thing for us, that they without us should not be made perfect (Heb. 11:32-40).

Paul had a congregation to care for. In spite of the evil he knew he'd find among the congregation at Corinth, he had faith in God, which gave him faith in people. He never gave up on people, although on many occasions he got sharp with them with "Thus saith the Lord." His task was the daily care for the saints of God. "Beside those things that are without, that which cometh upon me daily, the care of all the churches" (2 Cor. 11:28). Preaching preachers must care. This must be a daily concern. The saints deserve it; God demands it.

Paul acquaints us with a man in Christ by way of an epistle to the church at Corinth. "I knew a man in Christ above fourteen years ago, (whether in the body, I cannot tell; or whether out of the body, I cannot tell: God knoweth;) . . . How that he was caught up into paradise, and heard unspeakable words, which it is not lawful for a man to utter" (2 Cor. 12:2,4).

Paul does not neglect to tell us how heaven had to help him after this out-of-this-world experience.

> And lest I should be exalted above measure through the abundance of the revelations; there was given to me a thorn in the flesh, the messenger of Satan to buffet me, lest I should be exalted above measure. For this thing I besought the Lord thrice, that it might depart from me. And he said unto me, My grace is sufficient for thee: for my strength is made perfect in weakness. Most gladly therefore will I rather glory in my infirmities, that the power of Christ may rest upon me. Therefore, I take pleasure in infirmities, in reproaches, in necessities, in persecutions, in distresses for Christ's sake: for when I am weak, then am I strong (vv. 7-10).

Paul was indeed a preaching preacher who cared for the congregation. Preaching preachers this wide world over must care for the congregation. The Holy Ghost has made you the overseer. We must love the saints of God daily. This is our sacred trust and task.

We have this treasure in earthen vessels. These vessels are weak. Many of them are afflicted with various thorns which are commonly known to all people. Many preaching preachers have spiritual limps as had the apostle Paul. But that same grace that kept him from falling will keep us from falling. That same grace that enticed him to fight a good fight will entice us to fight on. That same grace that kept him running the race with patience will keep us running while looking unto Jesus. That same grace that enabled him to keep the faith will enable us to keep the faith. That same grace that granted him power to finish his course will grant us course-finishing power. That same grace that let Paul limp beyond the chopping block into an eternal morn where awaited the Eternal King of glory with a crown of life that fadeth not away will let us limp into that same everlasting day.

As I travel from place to place teaching, preaching, and lecturing to ministers, I admonish them, "Limp on, my preaching brethren. God's grace is sufficient for you." Yes, God's grace is sufficient for his preachers and his saints. Wherever the sons of men are serving the Son of God, God's grace is sufficient. Have faith in the God of grace, all ye his saints. Hope in him even as life's tedious trails lead you to the back side of life's mountain of trials and tribulations.

Because the profound preaching preacher has faith in God, he too has faith in the people of God. When he looks into the faces of his congregation, he sees the need of every member. He sees what they hope and fear; what they have allowed life's chastening rod to do to them and all theirs; how they have been tossed and driven on the restless sea of time; how sad and lonely they are deep down within; how they long to hear from heaven. The preaching preacher must meet these needs with a message from God filled with love and compassion.

The minister's message must be from on high. He has between thirty and sixty minutes, if that long, to lift these troubled souls out of the turbulent seas of trials and tribulations here in time and set them down in heavenly places. God's grace grants this.

By grace, the preaching preacher knows the plight of the people. He does not look down on them but rather looks up to God and intercedes, like Moses, for them: "Yet, now, if thou wilt forgive their sin—; and if not, blot me, I pray thee, out of thy book which thou hast written" (Ex. 32:32).

Might we ever be mindful that affliction was no stranger to the saints before us. Many stalwart servants of God had limps. Lot was Abraham's limp. Abraham realized this and one day had to separate himself from Lot. On that day, Abraham said to Lot, "Let there be no strife between us for we are brethren. Is not the land before us?" (Gen. 13:8-9, AT). Sometimes we must separate ourselves from our loved ones who are our limps.

Moses had his limp. His speech defect was his limp. But God's grace sufficed. Moses wrote the immortal prayer, Psalm 90, which is one of the most beautiful pieces of literature in the Old Testament. By grace, Moses limped on to Mount Nebo and fell asleep in the Everlasting Arms. God buried the old prophet, then buried his burial. On the mount of transfiguration, Moses appeared with Elijah as both prophets talked with Jesus Christ about the death he should die at Jerusalem. By the grace of God, the saints can live with limps.

Jacob had his limp. For many years, it hindered him. But then, one dark night, he met the Master in a still place. The Lord hurt Jacob in order to heal him. It was God's grace that let Jacob limp on to meet his brother in peace.

Oftentimes, years of obscurity have been the limp of many preaching preachers. Daniel is a case in point. He had had many, many years of obscurity. One day, the king of Babylon made a feast for a thousand of his lords. At the height of the ball, the king desecrated the holy vessels which his grandfather had taken out of the house of the Lord at Jerusalem. During this unholy act, the king saw the fingers of a man's handwriting on the palace walls.

It's amazing how providence puts prophets and potentates in palaces. The king was so terrified at what he saw that his knees knocked together. In his knee-shaking fear, he called for his royal wise men to come forth and read the writing and make known its meaning. The lucky reader would be richly rewarded. They came forth but failed. They could not read heaven's righteous sentence.

The king was frustrated by their failure. Here is a portrait in despair—embarrassed wise men, a frustrated potentate, a prophet in waiting, after many years of obscurity. Finally, he did what he should have done in the first place. He sent for the preacher. The preacher, who'd stood in line for a long, long time, was now at the head of the line. This was the preacher's hour. God's grace granted it.

Preachers must be willing to stand in line. Like Daniel, don't panic. Serve faithfully where you are. Do a good work. Pray, like Daniel, three times a day and all through the night. Prayer shortens the long line of waiting. When prophets pray, a three days' journey is made in a portion of one day. When prophets pray, fire falls from eternity into time in the twinkling of an eye. When prophets pray, the journey from a cave to a palace is a short one indeed. Daniel prayed. Now the years of obscurity were passed. He now stood at the head of the line.

Before getting down to the business at hand, Belshazzar had dialogue with the prophet. The king's flattery of Daniel was a bit lengthy. Having related the failure of his wise men, the King thus concluded to Daniel, "And I have heard of thee, that thou canst make interpretations, and dissolve doubts: now if thou canst read the writing, and make known to me the interpretation thereof, thou shalt be clothed with scarlet, and have a chain of gold about thy neck, and shalt be the third ruler in the kingdom" (Dan. 5:16).

In potentate-prophet confrontations, the potentate has always felt obligated to have the first words. True to form, the king had his first words; but the prophet had the last words. The grace of God provided for prophets to have the last say to and over potentates. "Then Daniel answered and said before the king, 'Let thy gifts be to thyself, and give thy rewards to another; yet I will read the writing unto the king and make known to him the interpretation' " (Dan. 5:17).

After the prophet had set the record straight he then got down to the handwriting on the wall. First he read: "MĒ-NĒ, MENE, TĒ-KĒL, Ū-PHÄR'-SIN" (Dan. 5:25). Then he interpreted: "God hath numbered thy kingdom, and finished it. . . . Thou art weighed in the balances, and art found wanting. . . . Thy kingdom is divided, and given to the Medes and Persians" (Dan. 5:26-28).

Here is a divine lesson for every preaching preacher to learn. Daniel, by the grace of God, came to the head of the line. He had been disciplined by the long time of obscurity, but now he was rewarded. He was dressed in scarlet, had a chain of gold put about his neck, and was made third ruler in the kingdom. Never mind your limps—even if they are thorns in the flesh—or Lot-like kinsfolk—or years of obscurity. You preach the Word. God's grace is sufficient for you. Stand in line. You'll get to the head in God's own good time.

"There was given to me a thorn in the flesh, the messenger of Satan to buffet me, lest I should be exalted above measure. For this thing I besought the Lord thrice, that it might depart from me. And he said unto me, My grace is sufficient for thee: for my strength is made perfect in weakness. Most gladly therefore will I rather glory in my infirmities, that the power of Christ may rest upon me" (2 Cor. 12:7*b*-9).

As a boy, I was a victim of asthma. Many times, my dear mother stayed up with me all night long. She oftentimes propped me up on several pillows placed lovingly upon the back of a chair turned bottom up, top down. She would pray for the dawn, at which time asthma sufferers seemed to rally slightly. Two family physicians attended me when funds allowed. They did what they could. They promised little or no hope. They told my mother there was no cure for asthma. Both doctors died. A divine compulsion engulfed my soul to preach. I cried out unto the God of my salvation, "I shall preach all the days of my life if you give me breath enough." From the purple hills of eternity came a still, small voice: "My grace is sufficient for thee: for my strength is made perfect in weakness" (2 Cor. 12:9*a*).

I have pastored north of the Mason-Dixon line. From Springfield, Ohio, the Lord led me back to my native Mississippi. Many of my dear friends worried because I left that large city church to return to Mississippi. They admonished me not to leave Ohio and go back home. But the same God who let me preach in spite of a lifelong affliction, called me back to Mississippi. I came, and I am glad I did.

My pastorate is a small church in Monticello, Mississippi, in Lawrence County. It is the only full-time black church of any denomination in that county. This is a historical fact and a unique distinction. But I shall not boast of this thing. I am also the dean of Natchez Junior College which is owned and operated by the General Missionary Baptist State Convention of Mississippi. It is my privilege to teach young students Old and New Testament and address them in the chapel of the little college on the banks of the mighty Mississippi River. Nor shall I boast or glory in this. Like the apostle of old, "Most gladly therefore will I rather glory in my infirmities, that the power of

Christ may rest upon me" (2 Cor. 12:9*b*).

Providence has provided a power to rest upon every preaching preacher. With this power resting upon us—like Paul in his time—we must in our time tell the divine time to the sons of men. "It is far on in the night, the day is almost here" (Rom. 13:12*a*, AT). We must and we shall tell them the divine time by God's holy sundial as by faith we watch the shadow of eternity fall across the shifting surface of mankind's turbulent trek from here to eternity. We must and we shall tell the saints of God that our ancient hope—the holy hope of our fathers—is about to come to pass. Our message to this troubled world must and shall be, "Be thou faithful unto death, and I will give thee a crown of life" (Rev. 2:10*c*). This is our hope. It is the hope of the world.

O God, Our Help in Ages Past

O God, our help in ages past,
Our hope for years to come,
Our shelter from the stormy blast,
And our eternal home!

Under the shadow of thy throne
Thy saints have dwelt secure;
Sufficient is thine arm alone,
And our defense is sure.

Before the hills in order stood,
Or earth received her frame,
From everlasting thou art God,
To endless years the same.

O God, our help in ages past,
Our hope for years to come;
Be thou our guard while life shall last,
And our eternal home.

Isaac Watts

3

God's Provision
for a Poverty-Stricken Preacher

1 Kings 17:1-16

The seventeenth chapter of 1 Kings opens like a Broadway stage curtain, and the prophet Elijah appears on the scene. This divine stage has been set by the outstretched hand of the God who created the heavens and the earth. Elijah, the Tishbite, who was of the inhabitants of Gilead, stands bravely and boldly before the king with a divine edict from God.

See a fearless prophet standing before a frightened potentate. Hear the prophet as he opened his mouth and declared what thus saith the Lord: "As the Lord God of Israel liveth, before whom I stand, there shall not be dew nor rain these years, but according to my word" (v. 1). With a short, sharp, cutting, to-the-point edict from God, the prophet, unlike the stage stars, did not bow nor take a curtain call. He left the stage as suddenly as he had appeared and disappeared, as it were, to the lonely land where God bade him.

How good, sweet, and profitable it is for preachers to hear the Word of the Lord, then proceed to obey the same. Trust ought to be the watchword of every preaching preacher. This is true because if you trust God you will obey him. Trust and obedience go together. To trust is to obey.

The big Book says, "And the word of the Lord came unto him, saying, Get thee hence, and turn thee eastward, and hide thyself by the brook Cherith, that is before Jordan" (v. 2-3). A most important point here is the fact that God did not bid Elijah to hide out of fear for Ahab but rather to hide so the "Eternal I AM" could provide for him. Elijah was poverty-stricken. He was well acquainted with the worst kind of inflation. A broke prophet was commanded to a cave.

Many preachers have been called from the big cities of their birth to go to pastor a small-town, cavelike church. Like Elijah, they trusted and obeyed. They were not doomed to disappointment. For, like Elijah, they had the promise of God who said, "Go and preach— and lo, I am with you." The "go" goes with the "preach," and then the "Lo, I am with you always" follows.

Elijah went. God called; the prophet answered. He relied on the promise of God. "Get thee hence . . . and hide thyself by the brook." Elijah went and hid himself. God spoke again to Elijah: "And it shall be, that thou shalt drink of the brook; and I have commanded the ravens to feed thee there" (v. 4).

It is my fervent prayer that when God calls some preaching preacher to go and shepherd a small, cavelike church in some small village, he'll move with righteous fear to trust and obey. Preaching preachers need not to be afraid to step out on God's Holy Word. His Word is bread on your table, clothes on your back, shoes on your feet, and money in your bank. His Word provides for the saints' every need. If his Word caused the dry bones to live, surely his Word will let the preacher live. Lo these many years, pastoring a small church, in a small town, in a small county has allowed this humble preacher to preach and live. The Lord of the vineyard has provided—he has given the increase. He continues to take care of me. He may one day call you from the cave to the city. But, as for now, concentrate on the cave. God is also the Lord of the cave.

Some of the most stirring sermons have been preached in small, cavelike churches in small obscure villages all over this world. Some of the great preaching preachers of this world today got their start in a humble, hutlike church in an obscure town or village. So, don't be discouraged if you are the shepherd serving in a cavelike church in a small town or an obscure village. Be faithful there. God is right by your side. He'll never leave you alone. He'll give the increase, and you shall surely live.

"And it shall be, that thou shalt drink of the brook; and I have commanded the ravens to feed thee there." Hear what the big Book says about Elijah's response, "So he went and did according unto the word of the Lord: for he went and dwelt by the brook Cherith, that is before Jordan" (v. 5). The obedience of Elijah again proves that it pays to serve Jesus each day. The saints of God who serve our Savior have nothing to fear. All we have to do is trust and obey. God will take care of his saints who trust in him.

The prophet obeyed the Word of God. The ravens brought him bread and flesh in the morning and bread and flesh in the evening; and he drank from the brook. Lo, a cave-dwelling prophet who dared to trust and obey God. Providence provided for this prophet. Providence has promised to provide for all preaching preachers and all saints who put their trust in him and who obey his Holy Word. Well has the hymn writer penned:

> What have I to dread, what have I to fear;
> Leaning on the everlasting arms?
> I have blessed peace with my Lord so near,
> Leaning on the everlasting arms.
> Elisha Hoffman

The saints of old leaned on the Lord. Our fathers of old leaned on him. Multiplied millions of believers all over this world are leaning on him today. His are the everlasting arms that shall never grow weary. They are eminently strong. Lean on him; he sustains his saints.

Elijah leaned on the Lord and lived. Even in a cave, one may lean on the everlasting arms. This is why it's so important for the preaching preacher to be faithful in the cavelike situations. Sometimes a cave-dwelling prophet runs into crises. We might as well face it; righteousness is risky business. But we have a mandate from God to tell the whole wide world that righteousness is worth the risk. Elijah discovered that righteousness was worth the risk.

And it came to pass after a while, that the brook dried up because

there had been no rain in the land. The preacher had preached a sermon to the king on the absence of rain. Now the message has returned
to haunt him in the cave. The brook went dry, and the birds rejoined
their feathered companions in the sky. This prophet of the promise
refused to yield to despair. Rather than looking down in despair at a
dried brook, the preacher of the promise looked up to the Dayspring
from on high. Instead of seeking after a wayward raven, the prophet
of the cave sought the One who makes the rose an object of his care,
who guides the eagle through the pathless air. Elijah looked up and
waited on the Lord who'd promised to sustain him. His waiting was
not in vain.

During my labor in seminaries and colleges, I have often encountered some young ministers who were quite impatient. Many of these
young ministers wanted large churches with congregations and sal-
aries to match. But they wanted all this bigness with little or no
preparation. One young minister who sought a big city church told
me he didn't put too much stock in education, nor did he go for paper
preachers (ministers who used manuscripts). In fact, he informed me
that he had never written a single line on paper, nor taken anything to
the pulpit but his opened Bible and his opened mouth. I need not tell
you that he is still seeking for the bigness he has sought. He probably
still has a long, lonely wait.

It would do young ministers well to remember, wherever you are
today, not to allow yourselves to become impatient. Don't ever have
a closed mind. And, for God's sake, don't be antieducation. If you
can preach without notes or manuscript, go to it! More power from
the Most High be upon you! But don't be antimanuscript just because you can't prepare or handle one! Do your college work! Attend
the seminary! Dig hard! Study your Bible night and day, day and
night! Pray without ceasing! Get your learning, your burning, and
God will give you your earning. And if after having completed your
training, you are called from the college city to the cave (small
church), don't slow down—move with confidence, hope, trust, and
haste. God will sustain you in the cave. Be faithful in the cave. After
the cave—the call to the city.

Oftentimes the cave is the anteroom into the city. The cave, many times, is God's divine proving ground prior to a preacher's promotion. A very timely and an important question to put to every young preacher is: "If you can't handle your divine assignment in your little cave, how shall you fare in the city?" God is depending on his preachers to be faithful in the cave. It might be that while you are laboring in the cave, God is courting a city congregation for you. God just could be making ready for you and yours a brand-new parsonage. Be productive and persevere in the cave. For after the cave, the call to the city.

And the Word of the Lord came unto him saying, "Arise, get thee to Zarephath, which belongeth to Zidon, and dwell there: behold, I have commanded a widow woman there to sustain thee" (vv. 7-9).

Sometimes, even the saints of God look hard upon the older ministers who do seemingly odd things at the command of God. So many times the saints seemingly forget that prophets are to obey God rather than man. Elijah did a seemingly funny thing. He went from a poverty-stricken cave—featuring a dried brook and a long-gone bird—to a destitute widow woman. When the prophet met the widow woman, she was gathering sticks to prepare a before-the-funeral meal for herself and her son. The prophet of the promise injected a dose of faith into the heart of the widow woman after her testimony of woe. "Fear not; go and do as you have purposed in your heart: but make me a little cake first, and bring it unto me, and after make for thee and for thy son" (v. 13, AT).

Preachers who've stayed close to God in a cave develop divine courage to make bold demands. Here stands in a city an old preacher from a cave, demanding that a widow woman who has only enough meal to make a cake for herself and her son make him a little cake first and then fix for her family. But the strange thing is she fixed first for the preacher. Elijah's words were firmly fixed in the widow's heart. His words were as a burning fire shut up in her bones. She heard them over and over again as she toiled in the kitchen which was almost bare: "For thus saith the Lord God of Israel, The barrel of meal shall not waste, neither shall the cruse of oil fail, until the day that the Lord sendeth rain upon the earth" (v. 14).

I can very well imagine that this widow woman actually hummed a tune as she meditated on the comforting words of the prophet as she obediently fixed for him. I can imagine also that Fanny J. Crosby had this widow woman in mind when she penned these lines in her immortal hymn, "Blessed Assurance, Jesus Is Mine."

> Perfect submission, all is at rest,
> I in my Savior am happy and blest:
> Watching and waiting, looking above,
> Filled with his goodness, lost in his love.

The widow woman worked in her kitchen, and God worked in heaven. The big Book says, "And she went and did according to the saying of Elijah: and she, and he, and her house, did eat many days" (v. 15). Saints ought to be glad to fix for God's preacher. There is a reward even for those who fetch the preacher a cold cup of water. The widow woman fixed first for the preacher, and God fixed for her. "And the barrel of meal wasted not, neither did the cruse of oil fail, according to the word of the Lord, which he spake by Elijah" (v. 16).

What a marvelous message! What a precious picture! What a wonderful lesson to learn! What a grand and glorious note on which the story ends! Here was an old preacher from a rural cave now sitting in the city at the table in the house of a widow woman. The preacher had been faithful in the cave. Now he's in command in the city. This is indeed a success story. From the cave to the city. From a dried brook to an overflowing kitchen. A last meal marked the beginning of many meals. One tiny cake became many multiplied cakes. God works that way. He works that way to perform his own holy will. When saints are faithful over a few things, God works his will so they are possessors of many things.

God is the great producer. Here is a divine show for saints and sinners to see. The stars are a poverty-stricken preacher and a destitute widow woman. The plot is exciting. The preacher flees from a dried-up brook to the house of a widow who prepares a little cake for a hungry preacher out of her last handful of meal. But the story ends well, on a goodly note. It ends with a blessed benediction from he who doeth all things well. It ends with a well-fed preacher and a compensated widow woman whose household did eat many days. It ends with an overflowing meal barrel and an unfailing oil cruse. There were more marvelous blessings in store for the preacher and the widow woman, but let the curtain close on the benediction scene.

The preacher did not despair; he prayed and waited. He waited after the brook had dried up, and the bird failed to feed him. He waited as the famine filled the land. He moved only at God's command. Now the widow woman's kitchen was filled with blessings in abundance. Saints ought to see God's grace and glory here. Even those fine missionaries on far away mission fields where supplies are scarce and poverty abounds ought to look up and be exceedingly glad, knowing that amid the worst kind of inflation, God still works his will. Saints all over the world must stand fast in the faith in seasons of distress and need. Your steadfastness is not in vain. Nor is your labor in vain.

Let preaching preachers learn this golden grace of waiting on the Lord. Though your charge be like unto a cave—a small one at that—be faithful and wait on the Lord. Though your once benevolent birds fly away forever, be patient and wait on the Lord. Though logic suggests to you that you should panic, don't do it, pray. Pray knowing that prayer is the key to the kingdom, and your faith unlocks the door. Though waiting seems to be a season without end, remember the words of Isaiah: "But they that wait upon the Lord shall renew their strength; they shall mount up with wings as eagles; they shall run, and not be weary; and they shall walk, and not faint" (Isa. 40:31). The testimony of the psalmist is also good to remember and rely upon: "I had fainted, unless I had believed to see the goodness of the Lord in the land of the living. Wait on the Lord: be of good courage, and he shall strengthen thine heart: wait, I say, on the Lord" (Ps. 27:13-14).

When the news of my departure from Ohio back to my native Mississippi reached a good friend of mine, he was visibly upset. We met at our National Congress in one of our large cities up North, and this brother expressed great concern that I was giving up such a large, city church to go back to the smallness of Mississippi. I appreciated the minister's great concern. But he need not to have worried. God commanded my homecoming. He has richly blessed my ministry both as a pastor and a professor. Many souls have been saved through my preaching ministry. Many lives have been touched through my teaching ministry. There are a number of stalwart pastors throughout the states of Mississippi, Alabama, Louisiana, and Tennessee who started preaching in my "preaching class." Other young Christian men and women whom I taught have gone back to their churches as directors of religious education, ministers of music, ministers' wives, etc. And the divine dividends go on.

May the ministers of the gospel of Jesus Christ be faithful wherever they are. Whether you are a cave-dwelling preacher or a big-city preacher, make sure you are a preaching preacher. Be faithful and up and about our Father's business whether your parish is great or small. As for me, my friend need not to have worried about my mission back to Mississippi. It was a mission. God commanded it. I'm so glad he did. God is here. He is with you wherever you are serving in this world today. Trust him and obey him. As long as I can live and move and have my being in him, I'll do what he wants me to do, I'll be what he wants me to be, I'll go where he wants me to go. When I was in sorrow's valley, he raised up my bowed-down head and started me on my way.

If Jesus Goes with Me

It may be in the valley, where countless dangers hide;
It may be in the sunshine that I, in peace, abide;
But this one thing I know—if it be dark or fair,
If Jesus is with me, I'll go anywhere!

It may be I must carry the blessed word of life
Across the burning deserts to those in sinful strife;

And tho' it be my lot to bear my colors there,
If Jesus goes with me, I'll go anywhere!

But if it be my portion to bear my cross at home,
While others bear their burdens across the billow's foam,
I'll prove my faith in Him—confess His judgments fair,
And, if He stays with me, I'll go anywhere!

It is not mine to question the judgments of the Lord,
It is but mine to follow the leadings of His word;
But if to go or stay, or whether here or there,
I'll be, with my Savior, content anywhere!

If Jesus goes with me, I'll go, Anywhere!
'Tis heaven to me,
Wheree'er I may be,
If He is there!
I count it a privilege here
His cross to bear;
If Jesus goes with me, I'll go Anywhere![1]

Note

1. C. Austin Miles, "If Jesus Goes with Me," Copyright 1908, The Hall-Mack Co. © Renewed 1936, The Rodeheaver Co. Used by permission.

4

God's Blessing
for a Broke Preacher

Acts 3:1-11

The third chapter of the Book of Acts opens with two broke preachers going up together into the Temple. They were broke, but they were together, going up to church, at the hour of prayer, being the ninth hour. It is an amazing commentary to see two broke preachers going up together, into the church, at the hour of prayer.

The big Book says, "Now Peter and John went up together into the temple at the hour of prayer, being the ninth hour" (v. 1). At the outset of my study of this verse, it struck me as sort of strange for the writer to state that "it was at the hour of prayer" and then add "the ninth hour." But after much prayer and sincere meditation, holy light illuminated my understanding. The writer did not mean for us to miss the fact that the two broke preachers not only went up together into the church at the hour of prayer, but they were also on time.

Full many a time a preacher will go to a prayer meeting during the middle or at the end of that service. But here are two preachers—God be praised—going up to church together at the hour of prayer—and on time. Thank God for this disciplined, Christian act by these two broke preachers here in the Book of Acts.

It is a wonderful thing for preachers to get together every now and then as a Christian witness to the world that ministers of the gospel of Jesus Christ can walk together. There ought to be a closer walk—a togetherness—between clergymen. The world is wondering why preachers can't walk and talk and worship together. The world is also watching preachers who always walk alone. Surely God is concerned about preachers who refuse to fellowship with other preachers.

Thank God forever for the two preachers who went up into the church together at the hour of prayer and were on time. God graciously glorified that hour and blessed that togetherness. He blessed it with a bountiful benediction. "And a certain man lame from his mother's womb was carried, whom they laid daily at the gate of the temple which is called Beautiful, to ask alms of them that entered into the temple" (v. 2). I believe that God bade the beggar's buddies to make a spiritual squatter of him within the very shadows of the church. This they did daily. They marred the morning's beauty each day by placing the spiritual squatter in the very shadow of the Temple.

Have you not often wondered why there are multiplied millions of spiritual squatters within the very shadows of all the churches and parsonages in this country and throughout the world? As a minister of the gospel of Jesus Christ, I firmly believe that God, our heavenly Father, has willed it so. Jesus cast his lot with the poor. Said he to a disgruntled disciple in Palestine one day, "For ye have the poor with you always" (Mark 14:7). These poor, spiritual squatters have "squatters' rights" to remain among us until we make them one or some of us. The Lord God who made all men has willed it so.

Many centuries before Christ spoke to the disgruntled disciple in Palestine, he bade the Old Testament scribe to pen: "He that hath pity upon the poor, lendeth to the Lord" (Prov. 19:17). That same scribe was commanded of God to say, "Blessed is he that considereth the poor: the Lord will deliver him in time of trouble" (Ps. 41:1). The Lord of life has championed the rights of poor, spiritual squatters among us. God our Heavenly Father has given poor sinners squatters' rights within the very shadow of our churches and parsonages in our parishes and church communities this wide world over. He has declared unto his church, "I am not come to call the righteous, but sinners to repentance" (Matt. 9:13*b*).

God richly blessed the togetherness of the two broke preachers. The spiritual squatter not only marred the beauty of the Temple but also begged and bothered those who entered into the worship service. The broke preachers encountered the beggar who saw them walking together and asked alms of them. It's amazing how the Lord provides. And Peter, fastening his eyes upon the poor spiritual squatter said, "Look on us" (v. 4).

What a grand and glorious hour that had to be: two broke preachers inviting a spiritual squatter to look on them. "And he gave heed unto them, expecting to receive something of them" (v. 5). Peter, who probably remembered the words of the Master, "It is more blessed to give than to receive" (Acts 20:35), said to the lame man, "Silver and gold have I none; but such as I have give I thee" (v. 6).

Peter realized that the man had money on his mind. But Peter had no money; nor did his preaching partner, John. But Peter also realized that the beggar's real need was not money. Silver and gold could not purchase what this lame-from-birth beggar man needed. The man needed dignity. He needed to be needed. He needed hope and heaven. The man needed the church, and the church needed the man; but he asked for money. The man did not have a money problem; he had a Master problem.

"Silver and gold have I none; but such as I have give I thee: In the name of Jesus Christ of Nazareth rise up and walk" (v. 6). With this golden gift certificate of God's healing and saving grace, Peter took the lame man by the right hand and lifted him up, and immediately his feet and ankle bones received strength.

> And he leaping up stood, and walked, and entered with them into the
> temple, walking, and leaping, and praising God. And all the people saw
> him walking and praising God: And they knew that it was he which sat
> for alms at the Beautiful gate of the temple: and they were filled with
> wonder and amazement at that which had happened unto him (vv.
> 8-10).

It was a great hour. All these marvelous things came to pass in the ninth hour. A lame man—lame from birth—leaped up and stood in the ninth hour. God's holy benediction graced this hour of prayer which was the ninth hour.

The great, preaching preachers of the past were men of prayer. These all knew that a saint who prays has great power with God. Daniel prayed, and lions refused to roar—let alone bite. Ezekiel prayed and saw a valley of dry bones. He preached, after he'd prayed, and dry bones lived again. Isaiah prayed, received holy fire from heaven and cried unto God, "Here am I, send me" (Isa. 6:8). Jonah prayed from the hell of the fish's belly and was delivered by God's outstretched hand. Jonah entered that great city of Nineveh, and what a sermon he preached! The city repented in sackcloth and ashes. The grace of God turned away judgment from the Ninevites and ushered in mercy and forgiveness.

The preaching preachers of this world must be men of prayer. In order to dissuade the lions of circumstance from swallowing us up, like Daniel of old, we must petition our Father which is in heaven. But not only preachers—families ought to gather about the altar and pray together and stay together. America needs to reestablish the family altar. Christian families this wide world over need to reestablish the family altar. The Christ of God says, "Men ought always to pray, and not faint" (Luke 18:1). Don't forget the family prayer—Jesus loves to meet you there.

God blessed the ninth hour of Peter and John in a marvelous manner. The ninth hour ushered a sinner into the kingdom of heaven. In that ninth hour, a beggar became a brother. In that ninth hour, a captive was set free. In that ninth hour, a nonwalking creature became a follower of the Lamb. In that ninth hour, that which had marred the morning became the glory and beauty of the day. In that ninth hour, God gave a broke preacher power to bless a burdened beggar. "Silver and gold," said the broke preacher, "have I none; but such as I have give I thee." It all happened in the ninth hour, the hour of prayer.

Every preaching preacher ought to set aside a ninth hour in his daily life. Preachers everywhere need to take time to pray. Praying

preachers are endowed with power from God to open up the Word.
Praying preachers are courageous preachers. They are brave
enough to encounter spiritual squatters on their way to their
churches at the ninth hour of prayer and make that hour a prelude to
a tenth and an eleventh hour.

It might be that God our Heavenly Father is waiting now to give a
broke preacher in the lonely parishes of the world power to go out at
the ninth hour and give Christ to that spiritual squatter who has been
squatting in the shadow of his church and parsonage day after day
after day.

The God who never slumbers nor sleeps, at this very moment sees
all of his broke preachers in their little obscure nooks, caves, and
corners. He sees you wherever you are in this world today. In every
state here in America and in every nation here on earth, God sees his
broke preachers. He sees, and he cares. He waits to bless each of you
just now.

There's a spiritual squatter in your church community. Don't
leave the poor parish squatter there. Give him the right hand of fellowship. Let him join the fellowship of faith. Transform parish squatters into saved soldiers. Fill the little charge with the downtrodden.
Broke preaching preachers, rescue those who perish, care for those
who are dying. It's the ninth hour now, the hour of prayer. The next
hour will be here soon, the hour of preaching. You might be broke at
the prayer hour. But the preaching hour follows. God has a love offer-
ing laid up for his broke preachers. After the prayer hour comes the
preaching hour. Aren't you glad God made you a preacher? Don't
forget, after the hour of prayer cometh the hour of pay.

As the lame man which had been healed held Peter and John, all the
people who'd been worshiping in the Temple ran together unto them
in the porch that is called Solomon's greatly wondering. Brethren,
we must be very careful when God performs a miracle through us lest
we become lifted up in pride and allow gullible gangs to make us a
cult leader. The danger is there lurking in the minds of people to
make you a cult leader after God has healed some sick soul by way of
a marvelous miracle through you. Be very careful when you're

broke, and God blesses some soul by a miracle through you. There'll be a gang of gullibles watching, waiting, and wanting to make you a cult leader.

Crowds are usually gullible after a great miracle has been wrought by the Almighty God. There'll always be a faithful few saints in the crowd who'll give God the praise and glory, but also among the saints, many times, are those who would make you a cult leader.

Some years ago, a young minister was pastoring in a county not far from where I served and lived. He was doing a really good job. But then after a great miracle had been wrought by the Lord through him, there were those in the crowd who bade him to become a cult leader. Those who bade the brother won him over. He did fairly well for a few weeks. But his makers soon tired of him and left their newly-made cult leader alone with a shipwrecked ministry. It is a sad sight indeed to see a preacher whom God has put on "short grass" because that preacher obeyed man rather than God.

All the people ran together unto them in the porch that is called Solomon's, greatly wondering. There's great expectancy here as a ripple of excitement runs through the crowd. There is a "making mood" here. Peter read the minds of his would-be-makers. Having so read, he set the record straight.

> And when Peter saw it, he answered unto the people, Ye men of Israel, why marvel ye at this? or why look ye so earnestly on us, as though by our own power or holiness we had made this man walk? The God of Abraham, and of Isaac, and of Jacob, the God of our fathers, hath glorified his Son Jesus; whom ye delivered up, and denied him in the presence of Pilate, when he was determined to let him go. But ye denied the Holy One and the Just, and desired a murderer to be granted unto you; and killed the Prince of life, whom God hath raised from the dead; whereof we are witnesses. And his name through faith in his name hath made this man strong, whom ye see and know: yea, the faith which is by him hath given him this perfect soundness in the presence of you all. . . . But those things, which God before had shewed by the mouth of all his prophets, that Christ should suffer, he hath fulfilled. Repent ye therefore, and be converted, that your sins be blotted out" (Acts 3:12-16,19).

When I think of how Peter handled this delicate situation after the Lord had given the ninth hour miracle through him, and how the fellow minister not far from my county handled his situation, I am divinely compelled to say one more thing to young ministers everywhere. Be very careful after God has wrought a miracle through you. Always remember, it is God's power used through you, lest you allow the mood of people to make you a cult leader. Preachers, preach the gospel of Jesus Christ, and he'll give the increase along with whatever you need. Don't let the mood of people mess up your ministry and your mind.

After your ninth-hour blessing, do like Peter, the broke preacher of old, who told people about a good God who sent his Son into this world to seek and to save that which was lost. Tell people who are moved to make you a cult leader, "How shall they hear without a preacher? And how shall they preach except they be sent?" (Rom. 10:14b-15a). Tell those who squat in sin—"sinking to rise no more"—"The word is nigh thee, even in thy mouth, and in thy heart: that is, the word of faith, which we preach; That if thou shalt confess with thy mouth the Lord Jesus, and shalt believe in thine heart that God hath raised him from the dead, thou shalt be saved. For with the heart man believeth unto righteousness; and with the mouth confession is made unto salvation" (Rom. 10:8-10). That's the story of salvation. It is the gift of God. It is eternal life to everyone everywhere that believes. Tell it everywhere you go.

Not so long ago, as we count time, a young mother who was a member of my church called me on the phone. She was distressed. She had a very sick, baby boy. It appeared that the tiny tot had some sort of birth defect which threatened his life. After having assured the worried mother we'd continue in prayer for her and the child, we did just that. All night long we prayed. All the next day we prayed. After several days and nights of the same, my wife and I decided to loose our faith and let it go. This we did. We let the Lord of life have our faith and have his way.

The Lord healed that little boy in a marvelous way. He gave that little lad an appetite which he'd lacked. Color came, and his pale skin became a healthy hue. His little eyes sparkled. He smiled happily. He played joyfully with his little cousins. He astounded doctors and nurses. He amazed the entire community and gladdened his mother's heart. There was great rejoicing at our house because God had wrought a miracle through the power of prayer.

The Lord comes by every now and then and gives his preacher a ninth hour. But after the ninth hour comes the eleventh. That Sunday morning following the miracle of the healing of that little boy, the hour of preaching came at the little church where I am pastor. I can remember a portion of the text that sabbath was: "When Jesus saw their faith, he said unto the sick of the palsy, Son . . ." (Mark 2:5). That Sunday we had an old-fashioned "Camp Meeting in Zion."

This was a most humbling experience for me. From this out-of-this-world experience, I increased my prayer life. I am endeavoring to have more and more ninth hours. I am seeking more and more spiritual squatters who squat in the very shadow of my church and my house. I try to get more and more of these off the squatters' roll and on the church roll. I strive to take them out of the rank of the squatters and put them in the fellowship of the faithful. Duty demands I do these things.

During some portion of each day I now steal away and seek a ninth hour. In so doing, I find that it pays to be alone with Jesus. I bid the saints of God everywhere to try stealing away to Jesus during some portion of each day. You, too, shall find that it pays to be alone with him. I bid preachers everywhere to steal away to Jesus during some portion of the day. You'll find that it pays to be alone with the Bishop of our souls. After the ninth hour the eleventh soon comes. Preach on, pray on, and press on.

Higher Ground

I'm pressing on the upward way,
New heights I'm gaining ev'ry day;

Still praying as I onward bound,
"Lord plant my feet on higher ground."

My heart has no desire to stay
Where doubts arise and fears dismay;
Tho some may dwell where these abound,
My prayer, my aim is higher ground.

I want to live above the world
Tho Satan's darts at me are hurled;
For faith has caught the joyful sound,
The song of saints on higher ground.

I want to scale the utmost height,
And catch a gleam of glory bright;
But still I'll pray till heav'n I've found,
"Lord, lead me on to higher ground."

Lord, lift me up, and let me stand,
By faith, on heaven's tableland;
A higher plane than I have found;
Lord, plant my feet on higher ground.

Johnson Oatman

5

God's Army
for an Endangered Preacher

2 Kings 6:1-23

The sixth chapter of 2 Kings opens with the sons of the prophets making a formal complaint to Elisha pertaining to their living quarters at their seminary. It appears that Elisha was a preaching president of the school of the prophets.

The big Book speaks plainly enough to this effect in the dialogue between the students and their president. "And the sons of the prophets said unto Elisha, Behold now, the place where we dwell with thee is too strait for us. Let us go, we pray thee, unto Jordan, and take thence every man a beam, and let us make us a place there, where we may dwell." And he answered "Go ye" (vv. 1-2).

One of the seminary students invited the president to accompany them on their benevolent journey. Elisha agreed and went with them. You remember how they came to Jordan and cut down wood for their precious project. You also remember that as one student was felling a beam, the axe head came off the handle and fell into the water. The young seminarian informed his president of his loss, including the fact that his axe was a borrowed one. You recall how Elisha was shown where the axe head had fallen into the water. And the Bible says, "And the iron did swim" (v. 6).

This was indeed a marvelous miracle. But poor preachers have been the agents through whom God has wrought miracles since time immemorial.

Here was an ideal situation for God to work a miracle. The picture here is of a poor preacher who is president of a poor seminary. There was also a broke student with a borrowed axe. If the student couldn't buy an axe, certainly he could not replace a borrowed one. So God caused iron to swim to the frustrated student. When the axe head was within easy reach of the amazed young man, Elisha told him to take it up out of the water. The big Book says, "And he put out his hand, and took it" (v. 7).

We often wonder what keeps a little, obscure, church-related seminary or college open year after year while seemingly on the brink of closing each academic year. God works his miracles and keeps the doors of our schools and seminaries open. "And he cut down a stick, and cast it in thither; and the iron did swim."

Brother college and seminary presidents, stay on the job. Don't panic. Don't despair. Don't quit. That same God, who put his holy power in a stick and made iron to swim like a tropical fish, is able to keep you from falling and keep the doors of your colleges and seminaries open. The temptation to panic and quit and go to an easier, more comfortable task with a better wage is ever present. But before I leave you, brother presidents, let me share this sacred suggestion with you in the wonderful words of a great hymn entitled "Yield Not to Temptation" which was written by Horatio R. Palmer:

> Yield not to temptation,
> For yielding is sin;
> Each vict'ry will help you
> Some other to win;
> Fight manfully onward,
> Dark passions subdue;
> Look ever to Jesus,
> He'll carry you through.

After the miracle of the iron swimming to the stick, the king of Syria warred against Israel. Again the man of God, through whom God had performed his miracle, served as the agent of heaven's holy power. Elisha was a preacher with supersensitive hearing. And his heart was in tune with the rhythm of righteousness. He was a preacher who walked to the divine rhythm of God.

The preacher is the channel through which God sends his power to perform miracles. Preachers need to keep in step with the rhythm of God's righteousness. Righteousness is keeping in step with the divine rhythm of God. Christ says, "If ye love me, keep my commandments" (John 14:15). Righteousness is the keeping of a holy rhythm.

Elisha had the secret. He kept in step with the rhythm of righteousness. So he who cut down a stick and caused the iron to swim was ready and able by the power of God to frustrate the Syrian armies.

Righteous preachers have always frustrated the enemies of God. This isn't new news; it's old news. Moses' young minister, Joshua, fought against the enemy of God's people. Nearing the end of that day's battle, Joshua got his "second wind" and needed only an extra hour of sunlight. He took a ten-minute break and called upon the Sun of Righteousness with healing in his wings. The big Book says, "God stopped the sun" (see Josh. 10:13, AT). Thank God for righteous preachers who have power with Almighty God to frustrate the forces of evil.

Anytime is a good time to frustrate the forces of evil. But preachers have a special privilege to use the divine power, at prime time, to frustrate the forces of evil. Sunday is an opportune time for pastors to frustrate the forces of evil. Every Sunday is a pastor's prime time. Pastors ought to always be prepared for Sunday's prime time. They ought to be in step with the rhythm of righteousness. They ought to be righteously ready to fight the forces of evil on the Lord's Day.

John, the Revelator, was himself a victim of the forces of evil. John was a prisoner on the isle of Patmos for the Word of God and for the testimony of Jesus Christ. John was in step with the tune of God's divine rhythm. John would testify to young ministers of the gospel of Jesus Christ all over this land and all over the world today. John would tell them to, "Get in step and stay in step, keep your ears divinely sensitive—listen in on heaven's divine broadcast. Hear his report of such a broadcast in Revelation 1:9-13.

> I John, who also am your brother, and companion in tribulation, and in the kingdom and patience of Jesus Christ, was in the isle that is called

Patmos, for the word of God, and for the testimony of Jesus Christ. I was in the Spirit on the Lord's day, and heard behind me a great voice, as of a trumpet, Saying, I am Alpha and Omega, the first and the last: and, What thou seest, write in a book, and send it unto the seven churches which are in Asia; unto Ephesus, and unto Smyrna, and unto Pergamos, and unto Thyatira, and unto Sardis, and unto Philadelphia, and unto Laodicea. And I turned to see the voice that spake with me. And being turned, I saw seven golden candlesticks; And in the midst of the seven candlesticks one like unto the Son of man.

Yes, John would tell young preachers everywhere and the saints of God everywhere to keep in step with the rhythm of righteousness and the miracle-making power of the Almighty will rest upon you.

Not so long ago I met a young pastor who was wearing a long face and had a troubled countenance. I asked the young minister what was bothering him. He informed me that he was disappointed and disturbed because he had preached very hard, but, try as he did, he was not able to reach his people. Finally, I asked the minister when he prepared his messages. "Late, late Saturday night" was his eager reply.

Here stood a young pastor who seemingly thought that the lateness of the hour on Saturday night had some sort of magical power in it. I took the troubled young pastor aside, and in a fatherly tone, told him that any hour on Saturday night is too late to prepare to feed the flock of God over which the Holy Ghost had made him the overseer. The time to start preparing for next Sunday's sermon is this Monday. The young minister took my advice. Needless to say, he did well. He was very happy the next time I saw him. He also informed me that beginning preparation for preaching on Monday for Sunday's sermon works.

I recommend beginning sermon preparation on Monday to all my preaching brothers. Sometimes an entire week seems too short for me. Many times, when the week seems short, I pray all night long with tears of sincerity. My prayer is, "Lord, if you don't help me to preach to your people on Sunday, I can't stand the storm."

Preaching without power on Sunday is a storm I cannot stand. I've learned, after more than a quarter of a century of preaching, that it pays to pray while preparing to preach. I've also learned this: you don't pond-fish yourself hot for preaching. Nor do you rest and relax yourself hot for preaching. You pray yourself hot for preaching. Fishing is fine. Rest and good health habits are essential in the lives of all preachers, but you pray yourself hot for preaching.

I strongly admonish all preachers to rest during some portion of every day, whenever possible. Fish in the pond whenever it's feasible. Relax often. But by all means, take time out to pray. For when you earnestly, fervently pray, you are seeking, knocking, asking; and it shall be found, opened, and given. So says the Lord of life. When you pray, you are preparing to frustrate the forces of evil.

Elisha was a praying prophet. Because he prayed, he was able to hear what the Syrian king planned militarily with his cabinet members in his royal bedchamber. Elisha relayed all of the Syrian King's military strategies to the king of Israel. The king of Israel saved himself, his soldiers, and his subjects several seasons because his pastor had heavenly hearing.

Only a preacher who is walking a holy rhythm of righteousness can obtain heavenly hearing. Elisha walked to the rhythmic beat of a divine cadence. He kept in step through prayer. He was a praying preacher who possessed heavenly hearing. So sensitive was his hearing that it distressed the king of Syria.

Prophets have always distressed potentates. The world today needs more potentate-distressing preachers. There are some potentates among us today who need disturbing by prophets who walk with God. Only those prophets with heavenly hearing can disturb those potentates who are troubling this world.

Elisha had no fear of facing a potentate. One lone prophet stood in righteous readiness to face all of the military might of the Syrian King. The potentate had enough military power—more than enough—to hurl at the lone prophet like lightning in the night. And yet the prophet stood his holy ground—kept on praying and hearing—and told Israel's king the plans of Syria's king.

Prayer makes ministers bold and brave. Daniel's prayer life gave him boldness to face a pack of caged, hungry lions. Prayer kept Daniel in perfect peace all night long in a dreadful lion's den. Prayer opened the den's door and set the prophet free. Prayer stood Daniel before an erring potentate whom he told: "Let thy gifts be to thyself, and give thy rewards to another ... Thou art weighed in the balances, and art found wanting" (Dan. 5:17,27). Prayer put a chain of gold about his neck and made him the third ruler in the Babylonian kingdom.

The story of any praying preacher is a success story to God. There may be risks, but righteousness is worth the risks. There may be many hard tests and many dangerous confrontations, but the praying prophet will come through.

Elisha, the praying prophet, pitted his heavenly hearing against the military might of a potentate. This within itself is a marvelous miracle. The heavenly hearing of a lone prophet saved the king and the people of Israel from defeat at the hands of a mighty, military aggressor. This frustrated the Syrian king. It necessitated him calling an emergency meeting with his top-ranking, military advisers. Behind closed doors, at a top secret meeting, the King let his hot displeasure be known to his top brass as he asked, "Will ye not shew me which of us is for the king of Israel?" (v. 11).

The King was wrong in his assumption. His reasoning was faulty. What he was saying in essence was: "Our top military secrets—our plans of attack—are being leaked by one of us to the king of Israel. As your commander in chief, I want you to show me the guilty one. That's an executive order."

An alert military adviser replied to the angry king, "None, my lord, O King: but Elisha, the prophet that is in Israel, telleth the king of Israel the words that thou speakest in thy bedchamber" (v. 12). Being momentarily relieved, the king commanded that a spy be sent out on a top secret mission to locate the abode of the prophet. With mission accomplished, the report to his majesty the king read: "Behold, he is in Dothan" (v. 13).

With crack military precision, the Syrian combat unit completely surrounded the city of Dothan. The Syrian soldiers cut off every avenue of escape. They came by night in order to launch an attack by day.

"And when the servant of the man of God was risen early, and gone forth, behold, an host compassed the city both with horses and chariots" (v. 15). Seeing soldiers surrounding the city, the young man retreated hastily to the prophet and reported on the situation. He wanted some serious answers to some serious questions, "What shall we do? Our escape routes are cut off. We are completely surrounded. There's no way out. There are many of them; only two of us. What shall we do?" (See v. 15b, AT.)

The young man was most perplexed by their dilemma. He wanted an answer, and he wanted it quickly. His heart pounded; his pulse quickened; he gasped for breath. The prophet did not panic. He did not worry. He did not despair. He remained cool, calm, and confident. The prophet not only had heavenly hearing, he also had heavenly vision. He turned on his heavenly sight and took a quick spiritual survey of the situation. What he saw satisfied him mightily. He turned to the young man and said, "Fear not: for they that be with us are more than they that be with them" (v. 16). The big Book says, "And Elisha prayed" (v. 17). The prophet didn't panic; he prayed.

Here is a lesson for all saints to learn. In time of trouble—when the way seems all hedged up and there's no escape from trying circumstances which threaten to swallow you up—don't panic; pray. In his immortal hymn, "Sweet Hour of Prayer," W. W. Walford shows the saints of God an escape route of faith:

> In seasons of distress and grief,
> My soul has often found relief,
> And oft escaped the tempter's snare
> By thy return, sweet hour of prayer.

The saints of God ought to remember that regardless of how dark and seemingly hopeless the situation appears, they can always take it to the Lord in prayer.

The prophet Elisha did not panic; he prayed. And what a childlike prayer the preacher prayed with such a childlike faith! "Lord, I pray thee, open his eyes, that he may see" (v. 17). The prophet asked God to show the young man what he himself had already seen. The prophet asked not for himself but for the sake of the young man. The prophet knew what God had dispatched from on high; the young man did not. The prophet stood confidently in the safety zone of faith; the young man stood on the sinking sand of doubt and fear. Well did the prophet pray, "Lord, open his eyes that he may see."

During my many travels from city to city and from state to state, I often have an opportunity to admonish the older ministers to be patient with young ministers who sometimes have a tendency to panic under sudden stressful situations. I admonish the veteran ministers all over this land to be kind to and patient with young ministers who panic. When they panic, you pray. Pray as Elisha prayed. God has respect for praying, veteran preachers who exercise their faith and make petition for young preachers.

The same holds true for the veteran saints who pray for young Christians among us today. Our churches would be far more effective and productive spiritually if our church mothers, our deaconesses, our widows, and other veterans of the cross would pool their spiritual resources and pray mightily for the young (babes in Christ) among us. The deacons and the trustees and the other veteran lay leaders of our churches ought to join forces and form a mighty prayer band on behalf of the young folk among the flock of God.

To pray for our young preachers, young adults, and youth in our church is far more profitable than condemning or criticizing them. It's a fine thing to keep in mind that we veteran saints were young, once upon a time. It would also do the old veteran saints well to remember that all have sinned and come far short of the glory of God. May God grant us grace never to forget that we too panicked and some old soldiers of the cross prayed for us until we came through.

One of the greatest spiritual impressions made upon my life was during my childhood days. I remember hearing my mother and my father calling my name in prayer when they thought I was asleep at night. Even today, when the way seems dark and the road seems long, I relive those Mississippi nights when my parents pooled their spiritual resources and called my name to God in prayer. This gives me strength to run on and tell the story of Jesus and his love.

If you are an old veteran of the cross, and you happen to know some young souls who stand in the need of prayer, why not bow right now and ask the Savior to help them to see. Thank God, my mother and my father bowed and prayed for me.

The Holy Writ says, "And the Lord opened the eyes of the young man; and he saw: and, behold, the mountain was full of horses and chariots of fire round about Elisha" (v. 17). What an amazing sight the young man saw! He gazed in profound amazement at heavenly horses and chariots of fire. What an unforgettable sight to behold. The young man saw what kings of vast domains desired to see. Thank God for the old veteran, praying prophet. And thank God for those old veteran saints of God, this wide world over, who bow and pray for young saints to see.

The young man whose eyes were opened by the prayers of the prophet saw the armies of the living God. These were standing in readiness to fight, if necessary. But fighting wasn't necessary. One angel could have done all the fighting. But fighting was not needed here. The heavenly unit had been dispatched by God to protect the prophet and to drive away the fears of the young man.

Young preachers, take courage! God sees you, and he cares for you. Young saints, fresh courage take. God sees you, and surely he cares for you. Children, trust in God and obey his commandments. He sees you, and he loves and cares for you. His voice comes down through the corridors of time, tenderly and touchingly saying to veteran servants of the cross, "Suffer the little children to come unto me, and forbid them not: for of such is the kingdom of God" (Mark

10:14). Civilla D. Martin had keen insight into God's care for all of
his children all of the time and penned:

God Will Take Care of You

> Be not dismayed whate'er betide,
> God will take care of you;
> Beneath His wings of love abide,
> God will take care of you.
>
> Thro' days of toil when heart doth fail,
> God will take care of you;
> When dangers fierce your path assail,
> God will take care of you.
>
> All you may need He will provide,
> God will take care of you;
> Nothing you ask will be denied,
> God will take care of you.
>
> No matter what may be the test,
> God will take care of you;
> Lean, weary one, upon His breast,
> God will take care of you.
>
> God will take care of you,
> Thro' ev'ry day, O'er all the way;
> He will take care of you,
> God will take care of you.

The young servant of Elisha learned in a moment of time that God
knows just how much we can bear. He learned in that divine moment
of truth that God will take care of his children—both young and old.
The young man's eyes were opened by the miraculous power of
prayer. Praying prophets have power through prayer. Closed ave-
nues of escape are opened when a prophet prays. Empty, desolate
mountains become filled with heavenly helpers when a prophet
prays. The young man saw and was strengthened mightily.

It is interesting to note that the presence of the angelic unit was enough to secure the safety of the prophet and the young man. No combat was necessary. Not a sword was drawn. Not a life was lost. Not a single soldier was wounded. Both friend and foe were saved from all harm and danger. Prayer protected friend and foe. Prayer brought heaven down to earth on a forlorn battlefield.

Heaven came to heal, not to hurt. Heaven came to bring peace, not confusion. Heaven came to draw, not to drive. Heaven came to save life, not to take life. "And when they came down to him, Elisha prayed unto the Lord, and said, Smite this people, I pray thee, with blindness. And he smote them with blindness according to the word of Elisha" (v. 18).

Here is another miracle wrought through prayer. A lone prophet prayed and captured an army that came to capture him. Blinded by the power of the prophet's prayer, the Syrian army was calmly captured by the prophet who spoke softly to his prisoners, saying: "This is not the way, neither is this the city: follow me, and I will bring you to the man whom ye seek. But he led them to Samaria" (v. 19). What a mighty God we serve!

Upon his arrival in Samaria, still another miracle was wrought through prayer. The prophet prayed, "Lord, open the eyes of these men, that they may see" (v. 20). The Lord opened their eyes, and they were surprised to find themselves in the midst of Samaria.

The king of Israel was most elated by the stroke of military genius of the praying prophet. He excitedly displayed his elation by way of an emotional question put to the prophet. "My father, shall I smite them? Shall I smite them?" (v. 21). The king was militarily moved. But the prophet moved by God's command. The prophet saw the divine rhythm of God in the series of miracles God had performed after prayer. His soft answer turned away wrath. "Thou shalt not smite them: wouldst thou smite those whom thou hast taken captive with thy sword and thy bow? set bread and water before them, that they may eat and drink, and go to their master" (v. 22).

It is most amazing how prayer sweetens preachers and people. The sweetness of Elisha was so contagious that the king of Israel could not resist it. The king caught the sweetness of the prophet. He prepared great provision for the captured Syrian soldiers. When they had eaten and drunk, he sent them away in peace, and they went to their master. The prayer of the prophet had such an humbling effect upon the captured soldiers who were now set free that they came no more into the land of Israel.

Down in Lawrence County at the church that I pastor, my members give me garden-grown greens in late November and early December after the frost has fallen on them. Those of you who are familiar with farm life know that frost makes greens tender and sweet. Before the frost falls upon them, they are tough and bitter. But after the falling of frost upon them, they become tender and sweet. Frost sweetens greens.

And so it is with the praying prophet and people of God. Prayer brings the tenderizing frost of God's grace which sweetens one's life. Prayer tenderizes and sweetens preachers and saints. Serve on, preach on, pray on, and teach on. The day of refreshment will surely come when the King of glory shall come and call us away. After our days of labor are done, then cometh the eternal rest and the eternal adoration and worship to Christ our blessed Redeemer. We shall see the great King in all his beauty when we've gone our last mile. Prayer will keep your soul sweet until the day of redemption.

My little daughter used to sing her Sunday School song for me when I'd come in weary from a preaching meeting. The lines were written by B. B. McKinney:

> Come, linger here with the Master,
> Come with your burden and care;
> Come with your sins and temptations,
> Whisper, oh, whisper a prayer.

> Come to your blessed Redeemer,
> He is the Saviour indeed;
> Call and He surely will answer,
> He will supply every need.

> Wait at the feet of the Master,
> Pray that His will may be thine;

> Wait, calmly wait for His power,
> Wonderful power divine.
>
> Whisper a prayer, Whisper a prayer,
> Bring Him your burden, Bring Him your care;
> Wait calmly here, Jesus is near;
> Whisper a prayer, Whisper a prayer.[1]

Down through the years, my baby's little Sunday School song has stayed with me. Many years have passed since she last sang her song for me, but I still love and reverence those lines. I often whisper a prayer, as my baby's song suggests. Prayer prepares me for preaching. So I'll whisper a prayer and keep on preaching. Prayer sweetens this humble preacher; it sweetens the gospel of Jesus Christ which I preach. Prayer keeps me strong and sweet for service. Even as I conclude this message, there is a divine urgency in my soul. A still, small voice whispers to me. The voice is calling me—softly and tenderly—to prayer. I love and adore the voice I hear now falling on my ear. It is the voice of the Son of God. I must and I shall obey his voice. The Bishop of my soul bids me to his throne of grace. He bids me come; I must go.

> Sweet hour of prayer, sweet hour of prayer,
> Thy wings shall my petition bear
> To him whose truth and faithfulness
> Engage the waiting soul to bless:
> And since he bids me seek his face,
> Believe his word and trust his grace,
> I'll cast on him my ev'ery care,
> And wait for thee, sweet hour of prayer.
>   W. W. Walford

Note

6

God's Care for a Crying Preacher

Jeremiah 18:1-10

Down through the centuries, Jeremiah has been called the weeping prophet. He was a bold, brave, fearless prophet who had a tender heart for his fellows. He had the unique distinction of being ordained of God as a prophet to nations. Nations heard him preach.

Jeremiah had many distinctions. He stood before prophets, priests, people, and potentates. Jeremiah suffered but not from a lack of preaching. He preached to preachers. The hugeness of his congregation caused him much concern. The sins of his own people caused him to weep. He was a prophet who was bottled up on the inside because of the burdens of his people.

Sin is a burden which is heavy and grievous to be borne by any God-called, God-fearing prophet. The sins which snared the people burdened the prophet. Those false prophets of Jeremiah's day also burdened him.

Jeremiah was concerned about the sins of his own nation first, and rightfully so. Being ordained of God as a prophet to the nations caused the load of Jeremiah to be doubly heavy and grievous. But, in spite of this, he was willing, after he'd been assured of his divine mission, to suffer for and with the people of God.

The first chapter of the Book of Jeremiah tells of his call, his mission, and his assurance. God's care for a crying preacher is included in this first chapter. Jeremiah was the son of Hilkiah, of the priests that were in Anathoth in the land of Benjamin. The record says the Word of the Lord came to Jeremiah in the days of Josiah, the son of

Amon, king of Judah, in the thirteenth year of his reign. The Word of the Lord kept on coming to Jeremiah.

Many times God's word must and does follow a preacher as he runs here and yonder on the highway of life. I've had a number of preachers tell me that God had to call them several times after the first call before they finally came around. God needs to call only once. It is his word that comes unto us again and again until we cannot help going and telling the gospel story. One call of God is enough. The divine urgency and persistency of his word which keeps on following the called person induces him to go.

God called Jeremiah once. God's word came to him many times. It came unto Jeremiah in the days of Josiah. It came also in the days of Jehoiakim, the son of Josiah, king of Judah, unto the end of the eleventh year of Zedekiah, the son of Josiah, king of Judah, unto the carrying away of Jerusalem captive in the fifth month.

Jeremiah, like many other prophets before him, offered excuses to God for not going the gospel way. These were readily rejected. "Then the Word of the Lord came unto me saying, Before I formed thee in the belly, I knew thee; and before thou camest forth out of the womb I sanctified thee, and ordained thee a prophet unto the nations" (1:4-5).

All God-called preaching preachers ought to remember, and remember it well, that God is the sanctifier of our souls. Time does not sanctify a man's soul. There are those among us today who contend that one must tarry—wait—and in time he will become sanctified. But God alone is the sanctifier of the souls of men. We don't choose God; God chooses us.

Jeremiah's argument was, "Ah, Lord God! behold, I cannot speak: for I am a child" (1:6). Jeremiah made his point. Then God made his point: "Say not, I am a child: for thou shalt go to all that I shall send thee, and whatsoever I command thee thou shalt speak. Be not afraid of their faces: for I am with thee to deliver thee" (1:7-8).

God made his divine promise to this prophet; then God touched him. The ninth and tenth verses of the chapter says, "Then the Lord put forth his hand, and touched my mouth. And the Lord said unto me, Behold, I have put my words in thy mouth. See, I have this day set thee over the nations and over the kingdoms, to root out, and to pull down, and to destroy, and to throw down, to build, and to plant."

Jeremiah was given the blueprint of his holy mission by God. The prophet was to rebuke the sins and evil of his day, but his mission ended on a merciful note. He was to build and to plant. Closing out on this divine note of love, mercy, and grace, God then reached forth and touched the mouth of Jeremiah. God sanctifies, ordains, calls, and touches. Whom the Lord calls, he qualifies.

Jeremiah did all those things God commissioned him to do. For a duration of time, he was the talk of the time. The merciful part of his mission was fervently carried out. His preaching planted and built up a righteous seed unto the Lord. It is the task of every preaching preacher to plant and build up a righteous seed unto the Lord our God. Jeremiah did this. Then a dark cloud arose over his ministry. Trouble came, and Jeremiah felt that there was seemingly no cure for the sins of his people.

At some point in every preacher's ministry, he has felt as Jeremiah did. He has felt that hope has fled from the flock. Sin does bring, seemingly, a hopeless situation in the land. But things are not what they seem if the people's God is the Lord. God has promised the preacher: "I am with thee, . . . to deliver thee" (1:19).

Full many a time, a preacher will let the burdens of the people get him down. Often times when sin has crushed certain of the congregation, a pastor will falter and fall beneath the load of pastoral care. Ezekiel once faltered beneath his load of pastoral care. But he too had the promise of God's divine deliverance. God came to his rescue. God called sweetly and tenderly to Ezekiel saying, "Son of man, stand upon thy feet, and I will speak unto thee" (Ezek. 2:1). God spoke to Ezekiel; Ezekiel spoke to the dry bones; and the dry bones lived again.

God cares when a glancing blow hits the preacher. Sin hits hard. Sometimes a crushing blow from the sins of saints glances off from them and strikes the preacher. Preachers must beware of glancing blows as they labor for the Lord. A glancing blow does not have the force of a solid punch. Nevertheless, it can deck one who is not expecting it. A prophet can be felled by a glancing blow when and if he does not expect it or know it is coming. This is a sneaky punch. This is also a preacher predicament. Satan is sneaky. He sneaky punches. He'll drop you, if only temporarily. Preachers must beware of the tempter's sneaky punch.

The downness of Judah momentarily decked Jeremiah. The miserable mood of the moment is set forth in the eighth chapter of Jeremiah:

> For every one from the least even unto the greatest is given to covetousness, from the prophet even unto the priest every one dealeth falsely. ... The harvest is past, the summer is ended, and we are not saved. For the hurt of the daughter of my people am I hurt; I am black; astonishment hath taken hold on me. Is there no balm in Gilead; is there no physician there? why then is not the health of the daughter of my people recovered?'' (vv. 10,20-22).

The awesome blow which struck the people of Judah glanced off and hit the prophet in his heart. He had a shepherd's heart. There's no hurt here on earth greater than that found in the heart of a loving shepherd. Jeremiah's heart hurt. Hear his lamentation from the awful hurt in his heart. ''Oh that my head were waters, and mine eyes a fountain of tears, that I might weep day and night for the slain of the daughter of my people'' (9:1).

As this humble preacher continues to study the ministry of this great prophet of the Exile, I am convinced that a prophet of the Lord has a divine right to cry. The crying of Jeremiah was a two-fold cry. He cried to sinning prophets, priests, people, and potentates. Then he cried (wept) because they kept on sinning. He cried (preached), and he cried (wept).

I highly recommend Jeremiah's twofold cry to preachers everywhere as I pass along. Preachers have a right to cry. They have a divine right to cry—telling people "thus saith the Lord." They have a right to cry when they see man's inhumanity to man. Prophets have a right to cry out against social injustice all over this land and all over this world. They have a right to cry when unjust people remain unjust—while proclaiming they are right and just. The prophet must cry out to nations of the world: "Love ye one another as Christ has loved you and gave himself for you" (John 15:12, AT).

Jeremiah who preached to nations used his divine right to cry. "Oh that my head were waters, and mine eyes a fountain of tears, that I might weep day and night for the slain of the daughter of my people!"

The prophet was faithful and kept on crying. A prophet need not cease crying because people continue in their waywardness. He must be willing to go back time after time and cry again, saying, "For the wages of sin is death; but the gift of God is eternal life through Jesus Christ our Lord" (Rom. 6:23). It's the precious persistency of the preacher which categorizes him as a preaching preacher. He must be willing to go back and cry out to sinners again and again. With eternal life with Christ at stake—prophets must be willing to go back to the outcast and cry out, "God loves you still," again and again.

Jeremiah kept going back. He kept crying out to the wayward ones of his day telling them—by the divine edict of God—"thus saith the Lord." He cried out to people and potentates. Jeremiah felt an urge to proclaim the gospel to potentates. Prophets of today need this same all-inclusive message from Jesus Christ our blessed Redeemer. The message of Christ is a whosoever-will-let-him-come invitation.

The world has become a tiny neighborhood. God gave us television. Cod has brought the nations of the world right into the dens of our homes. We can see and hear the leaders of the nations of the earth. We have learned how to pronounce their names. We know what part of the world they're from. Their folk are familiar to us. These are people whom God loves and gave himself for. The prophet has a right to cry out unto these potentates and peoples whom the Lord has brought into the dens and dining rooms of our homes.

God wants all people to live the more abundant life. That's why he came down here below. He came with a whosoever-will-let-him-come message to all people. His glorious command to "Go ye into all the world, and teach all nations" is still in effect. America might do well to send a preacher to those potentates who are troubling the world today. The big book depicts God sending prophets to potentates. From Moses to Malachi, the Bible depicts prophets prevailing over troublesome potentates. I admonish America to give her prophets an opportunity to become ambassadors of Christ to potentates who are troubling this world today.

I love America; it is my home. I'd gladly give my life, if needed, for my country. As a father, I diligently taught my children to love America and pray for her. As a college dean, I've taught my students to love America and pray for her. As a proud and patriotic pastor, I've always admonished my parishioners to love America and pray mightily for her. Wherever I go throughout many states here in this great land, I admonish people and ministers to love America and pray for her. Duty demands that I love my country, pray for her, and teach my fellows to do likewise.

The lines of the beautiful song "America the Beautiful," written by Katharine Lee Bates and loved by millions, is my fervent prayer for my beloved country:

> America! America!
> God mend thine ev'ry flaw,
> Confirm thy soul in self-control,
> Thy liberty in law.
>
> . . . .
>
> America! America!
> May God thy gold refine,
> Till all success be nobleness,
> And ev'ry gain divine.
>
> . . . .
>
> America! America!
> God shed his grace on thee,
> And crown thy good with brotherhood
> From sea to shining sea.

Jeremiah's willingness to go back and cry again and again pleased God. The prophet kept on crying against sin and corruption in the land, and one day God came and bade him to "Go down to the potter's house, and there I will cause thee to hear my words" (18:2).

The Bible says to obey is better than sacrifice. Jeremiah obeyed God. The record reads, "Then I went down to the potter's house, and behold, he wrought a work on the wheels" (v. 3).

As the prophet stood silently and watched the craftsman at work, he was fascinated by what he saw. The potter was in the process of producing a vessel. But Jeremiah noted a strange sight. The vessel that the potter made of clay was marred in his hand.

Clay which potters use to make vessels is manageable as long as it is damp. The potter must keep the clay loose by dampness. For once it dries, it becomes hard and thus unmanageable.

I've seen clay harden down on the Mississippi Gulf Coast, in my hometown, Gulfport, where the big ships come into port late at night. As a curious boy, I observed how the potter would fashion clay into a desired object. While the clay was still damp, he'd pour boiling-hot dye into it. When the clay had dried in the hot, Gulf of Mexico sunshine, you could not wash the dye out of the clay. Clay is manageable only while damp. The dampness makes it manageable and keeps it loose. But, once dry, it becomes hard and unmanageable.

People and potentates are like clay. They must be divinely managed before they become dried and hard. Preachers are commanded of God to cry unto peoples and potentates. Preaching is a matter of life or death. It's life unto those who accept the Holy One—and death to those who reject him. His Word is indeed eternal life to all those who believe. Peter wanted to know, "Lord, to whom shall we go? thou hast the words of eternal life" (John 6:68). And so he does.

Preaching is the hope of the world. The message of every minister all over the world must be, "Seek ye the Lord while he may be found, call ye upon him while he is near: Let the wicked forsake his way, and the unrighteous man his thoughts: and let him return unto the Lord, and he will have mercy upon him; and to our God, for he will abundantly pardon" (Isa. 55:6-7).

All people must be made to know the mighty God, the everlasting Father, the Prince of peace, before it is too late. Preachers must gladly go back time and again and tell people about the Son of God. They need to hear the good news of the gospel of Jesus Christ again and again. They need to know that, "Surely he hath borne our griefs, and carried our sorrows ... But he was wounded for our transgressions, he was bruised for our iniquities: the chastisement of our peace was upon him; and with his stripes we are healed" (Isa. 53:4-5). Joseph Scriven, in his popular hymn "What a Friend We Have In Jesus," has rightly said:

> What a friend we have in Jesus,
> All our sins and griefs to bear!
> What a privilege to carry
> Ev'rything to God in prayer!

Look at this prodigious prophet whom prophets, priests, potentates, and people feared and hated. Look at Jeremiah whom the Lord ordained before he was born, a prophet unto the nations. Look at Jeremiah who declared that the word of the Lord was in his heart as a burning fire shut up in his bones. Look at this courageous preaching preacher as he stands gazing at the potter as he works with clay on the wheel.

Jeremiah noted, with keen interest, that the vessel which the potter made of clay was marred in his hand. The prophet also noted that the potter did not despair, he did not panic, nor did he junk the marred vessel. The potter remained cool, calm, and confident. He knew his craft; he was a pro. Being a real craftsman, he simply made it again another vessel, as seemed good to the potter to make it.

The prophet Jeremiah is now free from the false prophets. He's free from wayward priests. He's free from potentates who turned deaf ears to truth. The preacher and the potter are in the same house. The preacher and the potter have become partners. They have become comrades for Christ. The preacher and the potter have started a seminary—one an instructor, the other a student. God brought the preacher and the potter together to teach the preacher a lesson, to lift his burden and brush the tears from his eyes.

As the prophet watched the potter remake a marred vessel into a perfectly whole vessel, God spoke to him, saying, "O house of Israel, cannot I do with you as this potter? saith the Lord. Behold, as the clay is in the potter's hand, so are ye in mine hand, O house of Israel" (v. 6).

I firmly believe that by faith I see symbolism here at the lowly potter's house—symbolism which is sweet, sacred, and soul satisfying. By faith, I see this humble potter's house as the local church of the living God; the clay, marred humanity; and the lowly potter, God himself. To this humble preacher, this is so wonderfully amazing!

We who preach and teach must get fallen humanity to the potter's house. Pimps, prostitutes, pushers, punks, dope addicts, wife beaters, child abusers, liars, cheats, backbiters, backsliders, the crude, the crooked, the criminal, and all sorts of sinners are welcomed, wanted, and healed here at the potter's house. Our task is to get marred humanity down to the potter's house.

The potter himself is the holy Host who heals. The potter specializes in fixing broken things. The potter is a fixer. He is a specialist—a craftsman who fixes broken things: broken hearts, broken homes, broken health, broken friendships, broken engagements, broken vows, and broken dreams. The potter turns no one away. Even potentates who are now troubling the world are wanted and welcomed and can be fixed for heaven here at the potter's house.

The potter invites all who labor and are heavy laden to come to the potter's house. Are you weak? Are you weary? Rest and refreshments are freely found here at the potter's house. Broken things are bound up here at the potter's house. There's peace and prosperity here at the potter's house. There's love and lifting here at the potter's house. No one is turned away here at the potter's house. Weeping preachers may come and find a tender wiping away of tears here at the potter's house.

Don't forget, America, that the potter specializes in fixing broken things. Let all the nations of the world come to the potter's house to be forever fixed. Whatever is broken can and will be fixed and made anew here at the potter's house. The medicine of mercy is found and freely given here at the potter's house. Thomas Moore, in the immortal hymn "Come, Ye Disconsolate," says it with such touching sweetness:

> Come, ye disconsolate, where'er ye languish;
> Come to the mercy seat, fervently kneel;
> Here bring your wounded hearts, here tell your anguish;
> Earth has no sorrow that heav'n cannot heal.
>
> Joy of the desolate, light of the straying,
> Hope of the penitent, fadeless and pure,
> Here speaks the Comforter, tenderly saying,
> "Earth has no sorrow that heav'n cannot cure."
>
> Here see the Bread of Life; see waters flowing
> Forth from the throne of God, pure from above;
> Come to the feast of love; come, ever knowing
> Earth has no sorrow but heav'n can remove.

Yes! Let those weeping preachers today come with their blinding tears of frustration to the potter's house! Let the wounded and the weary come to the potter's house! Let the bruised, the bleeding, and the broken come to the potter's house! Let prodigal sons and wayward daughters come to the potter's house. Once here, come boldly to the mercy seat, bow at the nail-pierced feet of the Savior and say with A. Pollard:

> *Have Thine Own Way, Lord*
>
> Have thine own way Lord!
> Have thine own way!
> Thou art the potter,
> I am the clay!
> Mold me and make me,
> After thy will,

While I am waiting,
Yielded and still.

Have thine own way Lord!
Have thine own way!
Search me and try me,
Master, today!
Whiter than snow, Lord,
Wash me just now,
As in thy presence
Humbly I bow.

Have thine own way Lord!
Have thine own way!
Wounded and weary,
Help me, I pray!
Power, all power,
Surely is thine!
Touch me and heal me,
Savior divine.

Have thine own way Lord!
Have thine own way!
Hold o'er my being
Absolute sway!
Fill with thy Spirit
Till all shall see
Christ only, always,
Living in me.

7

God's Message
to a Lonely Preacher

Revelation 1:9-20

The setting here is solemn, sacred, and sad. John, a lonely prophet of the Lord, is imprisoned. He is a prisoner of the Roman crown. Preaching brought him here. Had he not preached, he'd not be here in this awful place. But he had to be here—for the simple reason—he had to preach.

John had been with Jesus. John had lived with the Son of God. He had handled Jesus—had touched him with his own hands. John had heard Jesus tell the wind, waves, thunder, and lightning, "Hush now—peace—be still." John was one of the twelve who'd been most amazed as he'd witnessed a great calm out there after the Master of the sea had spoken.

This same John was there when Jesus fed the multitude with two fishes and five barley loaves. He had gathered up some of the fragments which filled twelve baskets. John had leaned on the Lord's breast in the upper room on the night of the Lord's betrayal. John had been with Peter when they went to see the sepulcher on Easter Sunday morning and found it empty.

This is the same John who was in the upper room both times when the Master had appeared unto them after his resurrection. John met Jesus at the Galilean meeting. John was on the holy mountain when the Master gave the Great Commission and then caught the cloud and went back to his home on high. John had stood there in awe as the angel came down from the heavenly host which welcomed the Master back to heaven. John had heard that angel speak, saying, "Ye men of

Galilee, why stand ye gazing up into heaven? this same Jesus, which is taken up from you into heaven, shall so come in like manner as ye have seen him go into heaven" (Acts 1:11).

Yes, John had to preach of those things which he had seen and heard. For preaching Christ and him crucified and risen from the dead, John was sentenced to spend a season in the isle that is called Patmos, amid the Aegean Sea. It was the Devil's Island of his day. Here he labored in the salt mines under a cruel taskmaster. The winds of the Aegean Sea chilled his body by night as the madcap waves dashed sickenly against the rocky terrain of the island's shore.

John was probably pastor of a church in the college town of Ephesus. It was from here that he was taken to the isle of Patmos. Far removed from his little flock, John probably reflected on better days when he'd walked the Palestinian roads with his Master who'd healed the sick, comforted those who mourned, and preached the gospel to the poor. He could still see that glorious day when the Master had taken the little children in his arms and tenderly blessed them.

John relived the wedding at Cana of Galilee where Jesus turned water into wine. John meditated on that memorable day when he'd stood at the grave of Lazarus in Bethany and heard Jesus call Lazarus back from the shores of eternity. John had stood in profound awe and amazement as the pallbearers loosed Lazarus from his grave clothes and let the man go.

But now John is alone and lonely as he reflects on those unforgettable days he'd spent with Jesus.

The saints of God have a history of making their burdens light by reflecting on the goodness of God. When our forefathers bore the heavy burden of slavery they used to lighten their heavy loads by singing, "I looked over Jordan and what did I see/Coming for to carry me home/A band of angels coming for me/Coming for to carry me home." "My Lord, He calls me./He calls me by the thunder./The trumpet sounds within my soul./I ain't got long to stay here." These songs made Babylon more bearable.

The psalmist has said, "I had fainted, unless I had believed to see the goodness of the Lord in the land of the living" (27:13). The saints of the living God have a holy history of making heavy burdens lighter and dark days brighter by reflecting on the goodness of God.

One Saturday night, as John reflected on those glorious days and nights he's spent with the Lord of life, he decided that in spite of his heavy burden of prison life, if he had the privilege, he'd do the same thing all over again. He'd leave all to follow Jesus. With the satisfaction of knowing that he had walked, talked, and toiled with and for Jesus, John dozed off into a fitful sleep. He was strangely awakened with a holy expectation early on Sunday morning.

This was to be a most memorable Sunday. His life never would be the same after this Sunday morning. John was not able to go to his little church at Ephesus, so Christ, the great Head of the Church, brought the church to John. The years have rolled on into nearly twenty centuries since the Lord came to John in the isle called Patmos on that Sunday morning. Still, we are given an account of the same by the precious pen of our preaching pal.

In the first chapter of the book of Revelation, John begins his historic account at the ninth verse:

> I John, who also am your brother, and companion in tribulation, and in the kingdom and patience of Jesus Christ, was in the isle that is called Patmos, for the word of God, and for the testimony of Jesus Christ. I was in the Spirit on the Lord's Day, and heard behind me a great voice, as of a trumpet, Saying, I am Alpha and Omega, the first and the last: and, What thou seest, write in a book, and send it unto the seven churches which are in Asia; unto Ephesus, and unto Smyrna, and unto Pergamos, and unto Thyatira, and unto Sardis, and unto Philadelphia, and unto Laodicea. And I turned, I saw seven golden candlesticks; and in the midst of the seven candlesticks one like unto the Son of man, clothed with a garment down to the foot, and girt about the paps with a golden girdle. His head and his hairs were white like wool, as white as snow; and his eyes were as a flame of fire; and his feet like unto fine brass, as if they burned in a furnace; and his voice as the sound of many waters. And he had in his right hand seven stars: and out of his

mouth went a sharp two-edged sword: and his countenance was as the
sun shineth in his strength. And when I saw him, I fell at his feet as dead.
And he laid his right hand upon me, saying unto me, Fear not; I am he
that liveth and was dead; and behold, I am alive for evermore, Amen;
and have the keys of hell and of death. Write the things which thou has
seen, and the things which are, and the things which shall be hereafter;
The mystery of the seven stars which thou sawest in my right hand, and
the seven golden candlesticks. The seven stars are the angels of the
seven churches: and the seven candlesticks which thou sawest are the
seven churches.

The message to John is clear. The Messenger comforts and as-
sures all preachers through this one lonely preacher out yonder on
the isle of Patmos. The Messenger clearly unfolded the mysterious
part of the message to the lonely preacher. The Messenger put the
parts of the divine puzzle together for John.

The Patmos preacher is told by the Messenger, "Fear not; I am the
first and the last: I am he that liveth, and was dead; and, behold, I am
alive for evermore, Amen; and have the keys of hell and death" (vv.
17b-18). The Messenger let the Patmos preacher know that all power
surely is his. Death was not able to hold him. It was he who'd wrung
the sting out of death and taken victory from the grave. With that
same majestic power, this same Messenger will bring about the ulti-
mate demise of death.

This is good news for all saints. Some are old and feeble. Some
have serious, lingering afflictions. Others are laboring beneath the
heavy load of loneliness. Hold on to God's unchanging hand. He'll
never forsake you or leave you alone. You are his child, and he cares
for you. You may relax and rely on his eternal promise: "Be thou
faithful unto death, and I will give thee a crown of life" (2:10b).

The Messenger stood amid the seven golden candlesticks. He told
the lonely preacher that the seven golden candlesticks are the seven
churches. Seven is symbolism. Seven suggests wholeness. Seven is a
complete number. Seven is a holy number. Seven is a perfect number. Seven then means that the Messenger—Jesus Christ—stands

amid all churches in this world today which bear his holy name.

Regardless of how down and out the local church may appear to the passerby, be it great or small, the Master Messenger stands among his own. He has declared, and he cannot lie, that "the gates of hell shall not prevail against" the church (Matt. 16:18). The church is in good hands. The church is in safe hands. "And being turned, I saw seven golden candlesticks; And in the midst of the seven candlesticks one like unto the Son of man" (vv. 12b-13a). Isaiah had spoken of him seven centuries before the Word became flesh. The intelligent, longsighted prophet wrote: "For unto us a child is born, unto us a son is given" (Isa. 9:6a). The saints are safe and secure. The church is in good hands. Well can saints borrow from Elisha A. Hoffman's song, "Leaning on the Everlasting Arms," and sing:

> What have I to dread, what have I to fear,
> Leaning on the everlasting arms?
> I have blessed peace with my Lord so near,
> Leaning on the everlasting arms.

Not only are the local churches safe and secure with their Lord so near, but the pastors (seven stars) of those churches are also safe and secure. "And he had in his right hand seven stars." Don't forget pastors, you are in the Master's hand, and no power here on earth can pluck you out of his hand. Christ said so, and it is so (see John 10:28).

During my many travels, preaching, teaching, and lecturing, several young ministers have told me how difficult it is nowadays to pastor and do a good job for the Lord with the hard "deacon's board" at their churches. Many of these young ministers inform me that these "boards" are so "mean." It's real sad that there are "boards" hindering rather than helping. But young ministers can and are pastoring the flock of God in spite of the mean, hard "boards." My advice to these young pastors is: "Pray on and preach on. Remember the One who has made you the overseer to feed the flock of God. Remember also you are his. You are in his hands." "And he had in his right hand seven stars." The Bishop of our souls has said, "And as ye go preach, saying, the kingdom of heaven is at hand." "Lo, I am with you." "Ye are in my hands."

John probably didn't have a mean "board" at his church at Ephesus, but he certainly had a mean, hard potentate. Prophets have a case history of problem potentates. Daniel had his, but he overcame by a divine power to read. Elijah had Ahab and the prophets of Baal. He overcame by a divine power to call upon a God who answered by fire from above. Elisha had his mean potentate, but he, too, overcame by a divine power to hear and to see. Jeremiah had many mean potentates to trouble him but he overcame at the potter's house.

I have the privilege to announce that God has given every preacher a divine power to overcome potentates and people who press. Trust God and obey him and he will carry you through. Whatever your special gift from God is, use it to the glory and honor of his holy name. Don't spend your time—which is so precious—fighting mean members and hard "boards." God sees and he cares. Look to him who said, "And, lo, I am with you alway, even unto the end of the world" (Matt. 28:20).

Many ministers have made fighting their major. But the major of every God-called preacher must be in preaching. Let the sweetness of Jesus in your soul overflow into your sermons. Let the love of Jesus which is shed abroad in your heart run from the pulpit to the pew. Preach the grand and glorious gospel of Jesus Christ our Lord in season and out of season. By his command, catch the season when the season comes in. There is a mighty power in this world to aid you. He abides with us forever. Let him lead you and guide you. He is able to give the pastor sweetness to steer and to serve in spite of mean "boards." Then one day the Bishop of your soul will promote you to a pastorate where your "board" will be kind and generous. This "board" will serve as your armor-bearers, strengthen your ministry, and be a blessing in your pastoral life. Don't be weary with your discipline of the mean "board." The discipline of the mean "board" prepares you for the blessings of the kind and generous "board." Pray on—preach on.

The one mistake ministers must not make is to spend too much time worrying with indifferent members. One of the soul-inspiring assurances Christ sent to the churches in his message to John was: "I know thy works" (Rev. 2:2). If then, God knows, and he certainly does, and if a man must reap what he sows, and very definitely he does, then the prophet ought to preach—first, last, and always. He ought to reevaluate the promise Christ has made to every preaching preacher, "And, lo, I am with you always, even unto the end of the world" (Matt. 28:20).

John's Sunday morning experience gives the saints of God fresh new hope and courage everywhere. Like John, we, too, may be in the Spirit on the Lord's day. My fervent prayer to God in glory is: "Lord, let your preachers and your people be in the Spirit on the Lord's day and be blessed as they hear from heaven."

John heard from heaven and wrote a message to the churches. A precious part of the message was, "Be thou faithful unto death, and I will give thee a crown of life" (Rev. 2:10). He that hath an ear let him hear what the Spirit hath to say. Be faithful in praying. Be faithful in paying. Be faithful in church attendance. Be faithful in missions. Be faithful in loving and lifting. Be thou faithful unto death. Let the saints of God serve on. Let preaching preachers preach on. Preaching, teaching, and serving days will soon be over. We have another building not made with hands, eternal in the heavens. The saints of old used to sing: "This old building keeps on leaning—I've got to move to a better home."

John, the Patmos preacher, saw in his Sunday scene, that "better home." He saw a holy city: a new Jerusalem, coming down from God out of heaven, prepared as a bride is adorned for her husband. He saw the light of that city—the Lamb is the light thereof. He saw a rainbow throne about the glassy sea where four and twenty elders cast down their golden crowns and cried "holy" to the Lamb. He saw the tree of life in perpetual bloom—the leaves of that tree are for the healing of the nations.

Those wonderful sights John saw should serve to inspire the saints this wide world over to keep climbing up the mountain. We'll soon reach the top. Faith will take us over. John saw the great King in his beauty who smiled on his children there. He saw this great King coming down, and his saints were coming up out of great tribulations, washing their robes, and making them white in the blood of the Lamb. The Patmos preacher looked heaven over and saw that there's plenty of good room in my Father's kingdom.

It is the divine duty of the preacher to preach the gospel of Jesus Christ to every creature. That means that ministers must make people free in every country in the world. The whole world is crying out to God-sent preachers saying, "Come here and help us." It is the divine mission of the church to prepare people for sacred service and to prepare people to meet our God. There is going to be a great camp meeting in the Promised Land.

Let every saint of God be reminded of his charge by the immortal lines of Charles Wesley written in 1762:

> A charge to keep I have,
> A God to glorify,
> Who gave his Son my soul to save,
> And fit it for the sky.
> To serve the present age,
> My calling to fulfill,
> O may it all my pow'rs engage
> To do My Master's will.

There are many faithful old veteran preachers all over this land and world. Many of these old veterans are here serving in Mississippi. There is a longing loneliness in your soul. Many of you here in this state have never moved from your first little charge. God sees you, and he cares. He knows your heart. He sees the old veteran pastor down on the Gulf Coast—from the Alabama line to the Louisiana line. Your footsteps are faltering; you long for a "better home." You've had your bothersome "boards," and you've had your kind and generous "boards." You've leaned on the Lord, lo these many years. Lean on him a little while longer—the day of refreshment will soon be here.

God looks in other directions. He sees those proud old pastors up in yonder Mississippi Delta—up in the rich and fertile flatlands. Some of you old veteran ministers have longed to head "North" by way of Memphis. You never made the move—you stayed "Delta-duty-bound." It's late in the evening—the sun's almost down. Make another round—old prophet of the Most High. He'll be here soon. As you slowly move up—God is slowly but surely moving down to meet you. The big Book says so.

And you old veteran shepherds up in the North and Northeast portion of Mississippi—preach on! The cold, cold wind from the Tennessee snowstorms won't blow on you in that fair land where you are bound. Old soldiers of South and Southeast Mississippi, serve on—preach the word another season knowing that the Day of Redemption draweth nigh. Let the old veteran preachers all over this world look up unto the Dayspring from on high. Today the building leans—tomorrow the move to a "better home."

Finally, there are Mississippi ministers way up yonder in the northern region of these United States who've grown old and feeble. You'd like to come back to the cotton fields at home. Many of you remember the Masonite plant, the pulpwood trucks, the sawmills, the soybeans, the shrimp and oyster boats, the seafood factories, the red clay hills, and the green grass of home. You might not make it back home here in Mississippi, but don't worry, don't despair. Make another round for the Master up there in the ice, bonechilling wind, and snow. He'll warm your soul with heavenly fire from above. "Lo, I am with you always."

I went "North" to pastor. I did my best in the ice and snow. The winter seasons were strange and hard on me—being from the sun belt of the deep South. With tears, I left a wonderful church in Ohio, the great Buckeye State. God was gracious. I made it back home. I am back now—back from the ice and snow to the hot summers and mild Mississippi winters. I am back amid singing brooks and sighing streams. But you old veteran preachers way up North might not make it back.

Through the Patmos preacher, God sends you a personal message of hope. The Christ of God, the Lord of life, the Bishop of your soul, has a mansion for you in his Father's house. If you don't make it back home here, you'll make it home to heaven. John saw that beautiful city with those walls of jasper, gates of pearl, and streets of gold. The Lamb is the light thereof.

There's A Land That Is Fairer Than Day

There's a land that is fairer than day,
And by faith we can see it afar;
For the Father waits over the way
To prepare us a dwelling place there.

We shall sing on that beautiful shore
The melodious songs of the blest,
And our spirits shall sorrow no more,
Not a sigh for the blessing of rest.

To our bountiful Father above,
We will offer the tribute of praise
For the glorious gift of his love,
And the blessings that hallow our days.

In the sweet by and by,
We shall meet on that beautiful shore;
In the sweet by and by,
We shall meet on that beautiful shore.

Sanford F. Bennett

8

God's Hope
for a Homeless Preacher

1 Kings 19:1-16

The nineteenth chapter of 1 Kings opens with King Ahab telling his wicked wife about the prophet Elijah's stunning victory on Mount Carmel. The king included in his account the sudden, shocking death of the 450 prophets of Baal. Apparently left out of Ahab's account was the fact that the prophet Elijah had given Jezebel's prophets first crack at calling upon their gods. He apparently left out also the part about the fire of God falling from heaven and doing divinely as decreed.

How strange it is—and yet it's not so strange—how men, unjust men, like to twist the good deeds which are done by faithful prophets to make them sound like evil. Ahab was careful to tell about the slaying of the 450 prophets of Baal. He was also careful not to emphasize the fact that God had answered the prophet Elijah's prayer by fire. Ahab had seen the marvelous miracle and could very well have testified to the same. But he chose the evil and forsook the good.

Elijah's mission had been accomplished. He'd pleased God and led the people back into the path of righteousness. The potentate also accomplished his mission. He'd pleased Jezebel and stirred up her hatred for the prophet of the Lord.

Sometimes when prophets and potentates clash, a potentate might win a temporary victory over the prophet by evil. But it is always an uneasy victory. It is never a lasting victory—only a temporary victory. God has so fixed it that the prophet always has the final victory and the last word. The prophet of the Lord has the last say over all potentates. The Lord has willed it so.

Ahab lost his bout with Elijah on Mount Carmel. So he retreated to his castle and rallied around a wicked queen-wife. He could not stand face-to-face with the prophet of the Lord in his bitter, humiliating defeat. In his weakness he turned to the wickedness of his wife as an unholy pacifier. His strategy was to set into motion the evil cunning of his wife.

Jezebel sent a threatening message to Elijah. It was a terse message designed to terrify. By tomorrow she'd have the head of the one who'd slain her prophets. She had a unique way of striking terror in the hearts of men. She had confidence in her tactics in terror. She was well versed in terrifying people. Jezebel majored in tactics of terror.

After hearing Jezebel's threat, the prophet fled for his life. He went to Beersheba and dropped off his servant there. But the prophet deemed it necessary to put more mileage between himself and Jezebel. Elijah reasoned that a good run was better than a bad fall. See how he runs!

Thinking as he did while running, he moved on another day's journey into the wilderness. His self-imposed exile landed him under a juniper tree. Sitting under the juniper tree, he requested that he might die then and there. The prophet thought that it would be more honorable to die there than at the hands of Jezebel in the city. He rejected the mere thought of dying at the hands of that wicked woman who'd run him out of town and made him a vagabond whose lodging was under a juniper tree. He is a prophet without a home. He is disturbed.

Note the distress in the prophet's voice, "It is enough; now, O Lord, take away my life" (v. 4). In his distress, the prophet forgot that God is merciful. He forgot that God is a loving Father who loves his children all the time. He forgot that God pities his people. He forgot that God is love—that he saves life in lands where mean men take life. He forgot that God is our refuge, a very present help in the time of trouble. And so he pleads with God, "Lord, I am done. Take my life" (v. 4, AT).

Many ministers since Elijah have had their juniper trees. There have been years of obscurity, like the case of Daniel, when the preacher is called in only after intellectual giants have failed. There are those ministers whose juniper tree is a small church with a hard "board" to contend with down through the years. Other ministers have sacrificed and have done their college and seminary work and have even gone on to receive an advanced degree at the university. Their juniper tree has been being a victim of a "meager-fare" honorarium. And, God knows, it's hard to live off a small-charge honorarium. Other ministers have labored down through the years at colleges and seminaries and have been continously bypassed at promotion time. These all have been distressed and have felt like the prophet Elijah. "Lord, I am done. Take my life."

The prophet Elijah was a vagabond on the run. He was homeless. He sat sadly under a juniper tree. But, as he fell forlornly asleep, heaven came and called on him. An angel came from the throne of God to comfort and care for the prophet. "Arise and eat" (v. 5) was the tender, comforting command.

It's amazing how the Lord provides. He is always by the side of his saints. Saints ought not despair when their lot is a juniper-tree experience. Saints need the divine discipline of the juniper-tree experience. The "always" of the Almighty included help for saints—even those whose lodging is under a juniper tree.

Jacob discovered that the "always" of the Almighty included a holy presence with one on a bare Bethel bed (ground) with a stone for a pillow. Jacob also discovered that the saints of God are never forsaken or left alone. He found that it's amazing how the Lord provides. After his never-to-be-forgotten experience with heavenly visitors, Jacob exclaimed, "This is the house of God; this is the gate of glory" (Gen. 28:17, AT). Whether your experience is a bare Bethel bed or a juniper tree, God is always available.

Elijah was awakened by an angel who commanded him to eat. The astonished prophet saw a coal-baked cake and a cruse of water at his head. He ate and wearily lay himself down again to sleep. The angel came a second time and touched the prophet.

Sometimes the poor prophet needs a second touch. The burdens of the ministry oftentimes gets so heavy the Lord has to give the preacher a second touch. The gospel journey is a long and tedious one. There are many, many miles of long winding roads to trod. Some lead to juniper-tree experiences; others lead to the bare beds of Bethel. But wherever the long road leads, God is there. Lest the preachers grow weary and faint along the way, a second touch is needed. Thank God for a divine second touch. Needing a second touch, saints sometimes sing from Lucie E. Campbell's hymn of prayer, "Touch Me, Lord Jesus."

> Touch me, Lord Jesus,
> With Thy hand of mercy,
> Make each throbbing heartbeat
> Feel Thy pow'r divine.
> Take my will forever,
> I will doubt Thee never,
> Cleanse me, dear Savior,
> Make me wholly Thine.

The angel came a second time and touched the sleeping prophet and said, "Arise and eat; because the journey is too great for thee" (v. 7). The record of the big Book is that the prophet arose, ate, drank, and went in the strength of the divine diet forty days and forty nights until he came unto Horeb, the Mount of God.

Prophets would do well today to learn a lesson from Elijah's juniper-tree experience. Forty days before, he was fearful and frustrated. Forty days before, he was doubtful and depressed. Forty days before, he wanted to forfeit his earthly life at the holy hands of the Almighty while sitting sadly under a juniper tree. But now he stood on the sunny summit of Mount Horeb. Forty days before, he sat on hopeless ground under a juniper tree. Today he stood on holy ground—Mount Horeb, the lofty mount of Jehovah.

It is so amazing how the Lord provides for his saints. The divine diet of God gave the prophet strength to come at last after forty days to Mount Horeb. "And he arose, and did eat and drink, and went in the strength of that meat forty days and forty nights unto Horeb the Mount of God" (v. 8).

Here in Mississippi, many ministers have small charges with "meager-fare honorarium." Some have asked me, "Dean, how long do folk expect a poor preacher and his family to live under a juniper-tree experience?" These ministers almost always refer to their hard and mean "boards." My answer is never flowery, farfetched, or eloquent. It is plain and simple. "Don't panic. Don't despair. Don't run away. Stay on the job and do your best in service for the Master. It isn't very far from the juniper tree to the mountaintop. Pray without ceasing and preach the gospel of Jesus Christ. Pray mightily for the sweetness of the Savior to saturate your soul. He has power to sweeten you and the sermons which you proclaim. The divine sweetness of his power "can change the leper's spots and melt the heart of stone."[1]

Twenty-five years of pastoring have taught me that Christ alone is the answer to "honorarium-mean-board" problems. A called-of-God prophet can pastor and do a commendable job in spite of the divine discipline of the "mean boards." The "boards" are changed by the sweetness of the power of Christ our Lord. His divine "all" and "alway" are capable of seeing you through. Ministers must never forget this.

The Savior who said "All power is given unto me in heaven and in earth" is he who also said, "Lo, I am with you alway, even unto the end of the world" (Matt. 28:18,20). This is the answer to my ministers' questions: "You won't have to stay under the juniper-tree situation always. While you are there, do your best; for God is with you."

This is true for ministers of the gospel of Jesus Christ all over this world! Your juniper-tree experience just might be God's divine escalator to take you up to a mountaintop experience, look up unto the hills from whence cometh your help. Let all the saints of God look up from the shadow of the juniper unto the hills of heaven. While under your juniper—don't forget the family prayer.

The prophet Elijah was moved from the juniper tree to the holy heights of Horeb. There he cast a wistful eye. The prophet became a cave dweller. A cave became the parsonage of a prophet. It is amazing how the Lord provides. He is always by your side. Your situation is his. Your extremity is God's opportunity.

A vagabond prophet, in self-imposed exile, a long way from home, was at home in a cave because God's presence was there. The God under the juniper tree was also the God of the cave. Where the prophet goes—in all the world—God goes with him. E. W. Blandy penned an inspiring hymn entitled, "Where He Leads Me." Well might all the saints of God sing along with those who preach from this great hymn of the church:

> He will give me grace and glory,
> He will give me grace and glory,
> He will give me grace and glory,
> And go with me, with me all the way.

God spoke to Elijah in the cave: "What doest thou here, Elijah?" (v. 9). The prophet took advantage of his audience with the Almighty. He told God about his perplexities. Prophets and perplexities are common companions. Elijah's reply to God unbottled the burden of his heart.

> I have been very jealous for the Lord God of hosts: for the children of Israel have forsaken thy covenant, thrown down thine altars, and slain thy prophets with the sword; and I, even I only, am left; and they seek my life, to take it away (v. 10)

Many times a minister feels that he is all alone in his perplexities. Perplexities do strange things to prophets. Perplexities have a way of making the prophet feel alone, forsaken, and threatened. But prophets are not alone. They are often threatened. But they are never forsaken nor left alone. There is One who never sleeps nor slumbers. He keeps an eternal vigil. He never forsakes nor leaves his prophets alone.

God commanded the prophet of the cave to go forth and stand upon the mount before the Lord. In that moment of truth, the prophet realized that he was not alone nor forsaken. Threatened, yes—forsaken, never! The big Book says:

> And, behold, the Lord passed by, and a great and strong wind rent the mountains, and brake in pieces the rocks before the Lord; but the Lord was not in the wind: and after the wind an earthquake; but the Lord was not in the earthquake: And after the earthquake a fire; but the Lord was not in the fire: and after the fire a still small voice (vv. 11-12).

The power of God's presence was the prime mover of the forces of nature. The power of the presence of the "Eternal I AM" caused a storm, an earthquake, and a volcano. These were distressing and perplexing to the prophet. But after these—a still, small voice. This says something to saints. It speaks clearly and distinctly to preachers. After the storms of tribulation, after the earthquakes of dangers, toils, and snares, after the fires of temptation, then comes the still, small voice of God saying, "Lo, I am with you."

"And after the fire a still small voice." The voice was small. The voice was still. The voice was sweet. The voice was soothing. When Elijah heard the voice, he wrapped his face in his mantle, and went out, and stood in the entrance of the cave.

A voice came to the cave. It had a familiar sound. The prophet recognized the voice immediately. He'd heard it before. He happily recognized it as the voice of the Lord. "What doest thou here, Elijah?" The prophet gave the same answer that he had given before:

> I have been very jealous for the Lord God of hosts: because the children of Israel have forsaken thy covenant, thrown down thine altars, and slain thy prophets with the sword; and I, even I only, am left; and they seek my life, to take it away" (v. 14).

Perplexed prophets ought to stand before God before they stand behind the pulpit. To do any task effectively—a task pleasing in the sight of God—a perplexed prophet ought to stand before the Lord.

While standing before the Almighty, the prophet can shed his griefs abroad. There God strengthens his prophets and sends them forth in the power and might of the Lord.

In the strength of the Lord, the prophet prevails. Prophets ought not to allow perplexities to rob them of their power to perform. Perplexed prophets are poor performers. And then there is a "Hand of power" for every perplexed prophet.

Ezekiel said:

> The hand of the Lord was upon me, and carried me out in the spirit of the Lord, and set me down in the midst of the valley which was full of bones. . . . So I prophesied as he commanded me, and the breath came into them, and they lived, and stood up upon their feet, an exceeding great army (Ezek. 37:1,10).

Ezekiel had been perplexed. He had been down, but God commanded him to stand upon his feet. Ezekiel stood before the Lord who strengthened him mightily. He preached a life-giving sermon, and the dry bones stood upon their feet. The dry bones became an exceeding great army for God! Perplexed preachers become preaching preachers when they stand before the Lord before they stand behind the pulpit!

After the prophet Elijah had stood before God, he went out by way of the wilderness, leaning on the Lord. Prophets need to lean on the Lord who died on Calvary. If you lean on him, he'll lift you up to great spiritual heights, and in his power you will perform.

The prophet Elijah leaned on the Lord. In the power and might of the Almighty, Elijah became a prodigious performer! He anointed two kings and one prophet! He became a maker of kings and a crowner of a prophet! The homeless prophet was now a king-maker! The prophet, now far removed from the juniper tree and the cave, anointed two potentates and one prophet.

Saints of God, and prophets of God, don't let your juniper tree and your cave experiences thwart and frustrate your performance. And don't think you are the "only one." God told Elijah, "Yet I have left me seven thousand in Israel, all the knees which have not bowed unto

Baal, nor kissed him" (1 Kings 19:18, AT). Knowing that we have scores of suffering saints as our sisters and brothers (many on far away mission fields) in tribulation, knowing that we are encompassed about by so great a cloud of witnesses, "Let us run with patience the race that is set before us, Looking unto Jesus the author and finisher of our faith" (Heb. 12:1-2).

It pays prophets to be patient. It might be that you've stood in line a long, long time in your respective field of labor. You have wondered, many times, "How long is this line?" Don't panic; pray and plod straight ahead! And as you go, preach, saying, "The kingdom of heaven is at hand." Never mind your juniper-tree experience with your mean, hard "board." Never mind your lonely cave of obscurity. For after the juniper tree, the cave; and after the cave, the mountaintop of divine deliverance.

Not from a juniper tree, not from a cave, but from a mountaintop, the prophet Elijah heard a still, small voice. That same voice is speaking today. It might well be that of the Bishop of our souls saying, "Fear thou not; for I am with thee: be not dismayed; for I am thy God: I will strengthen thee; yea, I will help thee; yea, I will uphold thee with the right hand of my righteousness" (Isa. 41:10).

And so it is with all the saints of God. Like in the case of Elijah, in time of stress and strain, trial and tribulation, God our Heavenly Father calls us to stand before him on the holy mount of faith. The angel of the Lord encamps round about the saints in their seasons of juniper-tree experiences. Then God himself calls us from our lonely caves of obscurity to stand before him on the holy mount of divine deliverance. Yes, after the storms of tribulation, after the earthquakes of danger, toils, and snares, after the fires of temptation, comes a still, small voice.

Grow Closer

There's a still small voice saying to me:
Closer, closer, grow closer to me;
In a whispered tone never leaves me alone
Closer, closer, grow closer to Him.

Oh I want to hear every message clear,
Yes I want ev'ry word to come through.
For if I make it in, I must walk close to Him,
Closer, closer, grow closer to Him.

9

God's Love
for a Disobedient Preacher

Jonah 1:1-14

Jonah stepped, as it were, from behind the curtain of a mysterious obscurity to the center of the stage of a divine action. Without fanfare—without any undue preliminaries—Jonah suddenly appeared. Unlike Moses whom we met in a homemade basket on the bosom of the Nile or the Greater than Solomon whom we met in a manger, Jonah appeared on the scene, in the spotlight, at the center of the stage, a grown man, a prophet qualified to do business for the Lord.

The Book of Jonah opens with the word of the Lord coming and calling this man who was the son of Amittai. He is commanded of God to go to Nineveh, a great city, and preach against the wickedness it had done against God. God told his prophet at the outset that the wickedness of Nineveh had come up before his holy throne on high.

What a marvelous opportunity for an obscure prophet. Most ministers, especially from an obscure rural rank, would delight in and jump at the opening of a big-city congregation. Scores of preachers have lived and died in the ranks of the rural. These fine ministers longed for a big-city situation. But they had to settle for the ranks of the rural. Smallness became their lot in life. They did well. They dutifully made the best of their small situation. They were comfortable because God comforted them. They have heard the final, "Well done, thy good and faithful servant" (Matt. 25:21). Now they rest from their labor.

But here is an obscure, relatively unknown prophet who is commanded by the Lord of the vineyard to go to Nineveh, a great city, and preach against her sins. In the command we see a unique promotion—from obscurity to prominence. The righteous Judge of all the world came calling upon an obscure, unknown prophet to come from out of the nowhere to the somewhere. Jonah's past is obscure but his present was to be of great prominence. Ministers ought to wait patiently on the Lord.

The glorious command to this obscure prophet is to arise and go to Nineveh, that great city, and cry against it, to tell that city "thus saith the Lord." The wickedness of that great city had come up before the throne of God. The time was ripe for preaching. The fullness of time had come. It was a matter of life or death. It was a time to choose life or death.

When we look at the need here plus the opportunity of the preacher, we cannot help wondering why the prophet went the way he did. The big Book says,

> But Jonah rose up to flee unto Tarshish from the presence of the Lord, and went down to Joppa; and he found a ship going to Tarshish: so he paid the fare thereof, and went down into it, to go with them unto Tarshish from the presence of the Lord" (v. 3).

Where does the erring saint or runaway prophet go to hide from the Lord? Former heavyweight boxing champion of the world, Joe Louis, when he held the title, had this to say about an elusive boxer who would soon challenge him for the title: "He can run, but he can't hide." And so it is with a saint whom God has sent on a mission of mercy. It is likewise so with a runaway prophet. He can run, but he can't hide. The saints of God often sing of his eternal everywhereness.

> Before the hills in order stood,
> Or earth received her frame,
> From everlasting thou art God,
> To endless years the same.
>
> Isaac Watts

At the command of God to go preach at Nineveh, Jonah rose up to flee unto Tarshish from the presence of the Lord. The prophet's reasoning was faulty. The psalmist said,

> Whither shall I go from thy spirit? Or whither shall I flee from thy presence? If I ascend up into the heaven, thou art there: if I make my bed in hell, behold, thou art there. If I take the wings of the morning, and dwell in the uttermost parts of the sea; Even there shall thy hand lead me, and thy right hand shall hold me (Ps. 139:7-10).

Jonah's reasoning was faulty, and his journey was both ill-timed and ill-fated.

It so happened that Jonah, in his attempt to flee from the presence of the Almighty, found a ship going to Tarshish. Note carefully, brother preacher, the prophet doesn't have to go too far nor look too hard to find the transportation for a trip of disobedience. That old wicked one, Satan, the old deluder, the arch enemy of God, and the deceiver of Nations, always reserves in readiness a vehicle to take the prophet on a trip of disobedience. Don't forget, the devil always has a ride for a runaway prophet. Satan constantly cruises in search of a runaway prophet. Any prophet who flags Satan's ship will certainly be accommodated. Satan will surely stop and let the prophet ride.

Jonah found a ship going to Tarshish. The captain and his crew were men who called upon gods which were spelled with a small "g." Be it far from this humble preacher to sit in judgment against Jonah for boarding this ship filled with sinners. Prophets ought to seek to save sinners. But this prophet had not been sent to seek these sinners. He had been sent to sinners, but not these. Jonah's mission was Nineveh. His message was to the Ninevites.

> But Jonah rose up to flee unto Tarshish from the presence of the Lord, and went down to Joppa; and he found a ship going to Tarshish: so he paid the fare thereof, and went down into it, to go with them unto Tarshish from the presence of the Lord (v. 2).

Jonah was not a broke preacher. Apparently God had blessed him during his obscure years before his call to the big-city charge. I firmly believe that Jonah had been faithful over his little charge. I also believe that that faithfulness brought about the promotion. Jonah had stood in line. Jonah had waited his turn. Now it came— sweetly and suddenly. He was providentially prodded. He was promoted. He was to run to Nineveh! He ran all right! But he ran the wrong way! The edict was, "Go to Nineveh."

As I go about my Father's business preaching, teaching, and lecturing, I often have an opportunity to talk with many young Christians. My advise to these young saints is: "Stand in line. Don't be impatient. Wait on your divine turn. God sees and cares. Get your training. Stay in school. Burn the midnight oil. Don't junk your education. Don't take the troublesome route of shortcuts." To young ministers with whom I chance to speak, I advise: "Be faithful in your little charges. Be patient. Be loving. Be kind. Get your learning, your burning, and the Bishop of your soul will give you your earning. Promotion Day will definitely come."

God promoted Jonah. From out of nowhere he was commanded to go to a large charge at Nineveh. Instead of obeying the heavenly vision, the prophet boarded a ship sailing for Tarshish. Instead of answering the call of God, the prophet became a runaway on an ill-fated ship. The Lord deputized the wind from his treasures. The big Book called it a "great wind." The Lord loved the prophet in spite of his rebellion. The wind and waves obeyed God's will. There was a mighty tempest in the sea. The ship reeled and rocked like a drunken man at midnight! The lightning flashed like a thousand lighthouses, and the thunder roared like hungry lions! The wind wailed like city sirens between midnight and dawn! The waves stood up like giant ghastly mountains and skipped like frisky lambs! With the wild beat of the rhythm of the storm, the ship appeared to be a goner to those on board.

So terrifying was this storm that the sea-hardened mariners were afraid, and the big Book says that every man cried unto his god. Here were pagan people praying. But as these poor pagans prayed, where was the prophet? The big Book says the prophet was down below fast asleep. Up on the deck, the sailors were working fast and furiously flinging costly cargo off the ship into the angry sea. The sailors lightened the ship, hoping the wind would blow them into port. But while pagans labored and prayed, the prophet—the one who'd caused the storm—was gone down into the sides of the ship and was fast asleep.

How strange it is that those who cause the storms in the church are always those who go to sleep during the storm. They start the storm—then leave the labor to those who didn't. The sailors toiled and called upon their gods. The prophet, who knew the living God— the God who created the heavens and the earth—was not calling on God but was fast asleep. Behold, the runaway prophet asleep amid a storm he'd started!

The awesome persistency of the storm induced the captain of the troubled ship to check and double-check his list. He commanded, "All hands on deck!" One was missing! Behold, it was the prophet! An endangered ship! Terrified, toiling sailors! One missing prophet! There was a pagan prayer meeting on deck while the prophet of God took a nap. This was how the shipmaster found the prophet—fast asleep down in the sides of the ship. See a sleeping prophet on a ship in a storm.

The shipmaster had a right to be sharp. A storm was raging. Sailors were busy. The shipmaster was on his job. But the prophet wasn't praying, nor was he preaching. He wasn't even counseling or comforting. He was sleeping. He was down, but not upon bending knees. He was down in the sides of the ship sleeping! "What meanest thou, O sleeper? arise, call upon thy God, if so be that God will think upon us, that we perish not" (v. 6).

The storm told the mariners a divine story. God works in a mysterious way, the storm suggested to sailors at sea. They followed the suggestion and decided to cast lots to determine who'd caused the evil to come upon them. They cast—the lot fell on Jonah. The storm suggested again. The storm whispered to the sailors that the drowsy passenger should be interrogated! They heeded the wind. In rapid-fire precision, the sailors hurled questions to the disobedient prophet. For whose cause is this evil come upon us? What is your occupation? Where are you from? What is your country? Who are your people? (See verse 8.)

With the spotlight of the sailors shining upon him, the prophet was now wide awake. Nor did he waste words. He was precise and to the point. He said unto them: "I am an Hebrew; and I fear the Lord, the God of heaven, which hath made the sea and the dry land" (v. 9).

Those few facts told by the runaway prophet amid a terrible tempest, had a startling effect upon the sailors. They were exceedingly afraid as the wind whispered to them that Jonah was wanted. The wind whispered that Jonah was a fugitive from divine justice. The wind whispered that Jonah was a storm maker. The wind whispered that Jonah was running from the righteous Judge of all the world. Jonah had told them, and the wind witnessed to the truth he'd spoken in the storm.

The sailors wanted to know much more. It's real sad when sinners have to pull preaching out of a preacher. My advice to preachers, all preachers, but more especially to young preachers is, "Don't force people to pull preaching out of you." The Bishop of your souls has commanded all preachers everywhere: "And as ye go, preach, saying, The kingdom of heaven is at hand" (Matt. 10:7). The sailors had to pull preaching out of the preacher. "What shall we do unto thee, that the sea may be calm unto us?" (v. 11). They had not caused the storm. They now knew that the preacher was the culprit. They wanted some straightforward answers, and they wanted them quick! A storm was raging!

The prophet confessed. Thank God for a confessing preacher! "Take me up, and throw me overboard into the sea; then shall the sea be calm unto you: for I know that for my sake this great storm has come upon you sailors" (v. 12, AT). The words of the prophet had a softening and a sweetening effect upon the sailors. They tried courageously to bring the ship into port. They failed. They failed because God had commanded the wind to arrest the runaway prophet before it ceased to blow. The wind worked against the sailors. They called upon the name of the Lord. And what a prayer they prayed! They prayed for their lives to be spared. They prayed for the prophet. They asked God for mercy. God granted them mercy. But this just God must punish and pardon the preacher. The grace of God allows for punishment, pardon, and peace.

The sailors took Jonah and threw him into the sea, and the sea strangely ceased from raging. The sudden calmness of the sea caused a godly fear to engulf the sailors. They offered a sacrifice unto the Lord and made vows. It's so amazing how the Lord provides! God granted grace to sinful sailors. God provided for a runaway prophet to preach on board an ill-fated ship and saved all on board. God granted grace and glory to a wayward, disobedient prophet. God kept on loving the prophet in spite of his disobedience.

Yes, it's amazing how the Lord loves and provides! The Lord had prepared a great fish to swallow up Jonah. And Jonah was in the belly of the fish three days and three nights (v. 17). This was the Lord's doing. It still inspires after all these years. The prophet had preached on board. Now he's overboard. But God had already provided for the prophet. The provision was not a big fish straying in a storm. The Lord had prepared a great fish whose divine mission was to swallow up the minister. The same God who'd deputized the wind also made a fish a missionary. With mission accomplished, Jonah was in the belly of the fish three days and three nights.

Those three days and three nights were very eventful and most significant. They were most significant for two very important reasons. First, in the belly of the prepared fish, the prophet would be punished and pardoned. Second, many centuries later, Jesus, the Lord of life, would refer to the authenticity of the great fish and to the fact that God is able to provide for his prophet. God can and did, according to Jesus, the Son of God, prepare a great fish to swallow up a prophet. One day in Palestine, the Pharisees teamed up with the Sadducees and tempted Jesus, desiring a sign from heaven. Jesus was grieved by their hypocrisy. He told them,

> When it is evening, ye say, it will be fair weather: for the sky is red. And in the morning, it will be foul weather to-day: for the sky is red and lowring. O ye hypocrites, ye can discern the face of the sky; but can ye not discern the signs of the times? A wicked and adulterous generation seeketh after a sign; and there shall no sign be given unto it, but the sign of the prophet Jonas (Matthew 16:2-4).

The sign Jesus referred to was those three days and three nights in which Jonah was in the belly of the fish. Jesus would be in the heart of the earth for three days and nights. Jesus made the similarity in order to authenticate the fact that God did prepare a fish—a great fish—to swallow up Jonah, the prophet. Jesus said that Jonah was in the belly of the fish three days and three nights. Jesus said so, and it was so.

God found his grace way to punish and pardon his prophet. That's good news to saints everywhere. God has a grace way which provides punishment and pardon. God punished the runaway prophet—then pardoned him. Now the pardoned prophet is on the dry land. The grace of God delivers the saints of God from the depths of despair to the dry land of peace and prosperity. Preachers ought to take advantage of this grace way of God. If you have gone contrary to his holy will, ask God to get you back into the path of light. His grace grants the same. His mercy is now available. If you've been derelict in your sacred duty, God's grace way is available to aid you on your way back to a spiritual comeback. If you've been sleeping on the Savior while others worked to weather the storm you started, pray to God for his grace way of pardon and peace. Then do as the prophet Jonah did. Make haste to do what God commanded you to do in the first place.

Nineveh was a great city. God called Jonah a second time and commanded him to go. He went. He made a three-day journey in a portion of one day. He hurried for heaven. What a preaching preacher was Jonah! How the preacher did preach! He cried aloud. He spared not. "Nineveh, you have forty days to prepare to meet thy God! Forty days and the judgment of God will be upon you! Forty days and you must meet the Holy One of Israel! Forty days and every secret thing will be made known to the God who made the seas and the dry land! Forty days and you shall stand before the Righteous Judge of all the world'' (author's paraphrase).

What a swift journey Jonah took! What a mighty message he brought to the inhabitants of Nineveh! Jonah went there according to the word of the Lord. Preachers everywhere ought to go on their preaching journeys according to the word of the Lord. When they do, they go out in the power and might of his word. When you preach in his power and might, things will happen that astound and thrill. Jonah preached, and people repented by the power of his preaching. People and beasts went softly in ashes of repentance. That same God whose grace punished and pardoned the preacher also punished and pardoned the people of Nineveh. Jesus told some critics that the people of Nineveh would rise up in the judgment and condemn them because the Ninevites repented at the preaching of Jonah. Thank God for pardoned preachers who preach to people whom God also pardons. Thank God for preaching preachers all over this world. In 1707, Isaac Watts wrote:

"Go Preach My Gospel," Saith the Lord

"Go preach My gospel," saith the Lord;
"Bid the whole earth My grace receive:
He shall be saved that trusts My word,
And he condemned who'll not believe."

"I'll make your great commission known;
And ye shall prove My gospel true
By all the works that I have done,
By the wonders ye shall do.

Teach all nations My commands;
I'm with you till the world shall end;
All pow'r is trusted in My hands:
I can destroy, and I defend."

He spake, and light shone round His head;
On a bright cloud to heav'n He rode:
They to the farthest nations spread
The grace of their ascended God.

                               Isaac Watts

10

God's Home
for a Departed Preacher

Exodus 3:1-10
Deuteronomy 34:5-6
Matthew 17:1-5

The courageous life of Moses still inspires the saints of God all over the world. Moses was a meek man. According to the big Book, he was the meekest man in all the earth. He was patient, kind, gentle, and long-suffering. He loved people—both good and bad—and bore long and lovingly with them. He often went beyond the call of duty for his people and interceded to God on their behalf when their wayward-ness seemed to be their undoing. What a remarkable man was this minister, Moses.

The prophet Moses seemed destined—from birth—for greatness. You remember he'd been born when an edict of Pharaoh had de-creed the destruction of Moses and all other Hebrew baby boys at birth. You remember also that the girls were to be kept alive. When Moses was born, his mother saw something strange in him. And see-ing this sacred strangeness, she hid the baby for several months.

It's amazing how the Lord provides! A potentate had made an edict that a prophet be cut off before he preached. Prophets don't preach and then be called. Prophets are called—then they preach. God told Jeremiah, "Before I formed thee in the belly I knew thee; and before thou camest forth out of the womb I sanctified thee, and I ordained thee a prophet unto the nations" (1:5). Jeremiah's santifi-cation and ordination came to pass in heaven before he was con-ceived. Prophets who were not born to preach were not sent—they went. God calls his prophets in eternity. When a God-called prophet arrives here in time, he does so as a born preacher.

The mother of Moses saw a sacred strangeness in her son. She hid him as long as she could. Apparently, the baby boy had preaching lungs. He cried loudly. When his crying could be clearly and distinctly heard in the house, his mother made a homemade bassinet. The baby bed was designed to float upon the bosom of the Nile. Then God took over. The saints have a sacred right to sing:

> God moves in a mysterious way
> His wonders to perform;
> He plants His footsteps in the sea,
> And rides upon the storm.
>   William Cowper

With Moses' sister Miriam standing in the shadows of the Nile, the daughter of the potentate came down with her royal handmaidens to bathe therein. As the princess walked into the water, she saw the basket and had her maids to fetch it to her. They opened the basket, and the heart of her royal highness was deeply touched by the sight of baby Moses. She recognized him as one of the Hebrew baby boys. And when the baby cried, it melted the princess's heart. God moved Miriam to speak to the queen concerning a Hebrew nurse for the baby boy. The princess granted Miriam permission, and the mother of Moses had the privilege of nursing her own child while receiving wages from her royal highness, the princess.

The plans of potentates are no match for the power of Providence. What potentates appoint, Providence can disappoint. The decree of the potentate was to kill Moses. But the divine decree of Providence was to save Moses. Consequently, the daughter of the decreeing potentate is the earthly savior of the baby Moses. She hired the child's own mother to nurse him and paid her royal wages for caring for the child. When the child had been weaned, he was brought, by his mother, and turned over to the princess who in turn raised him as a prince of Egypt. Unknowingly, she was a handmaiden of the Lord. She was preparing a prophet in the house of a potentate.

Truly, it's amazing how the Lord abides and provides. Prophets and potentates usually don't have too much in common. But Providence serves as a common denominator here. Both prophet and potentate, by the precious power of Providence, are able to abide together under the same roof and love each other as father and son. Only God can change a leper's spots and melt the heart of stone.

By the providence of the Almighty, Moses grew up in the very household of Pharaoh. He was trained in the culture of the Egyptians. For forty years, Moses had the rich experience of being educated in Egypt as a prince and practicing what he'd learned there.

Then Providence moved again in a mysterious way. Moses got into trouble and had to leave Egypt hurriedly. He fled to the land of Midian, where for the next forty years he was to train for his "wilderness ministry." It takes time to get ready to lead the people of God.

It has been my good fortune to preach, teach, and lecture to many young ministers here in Mississippi. Most of my ministry of a quarter of a century has been here in this state. My constant advice to these young preachers has been for them to prepare themselves academically for the task which lies ahead. Young ministers must not allow themselves to become impatient and indifferent toward their proper training in quest for the "big city church." Young ministers must keep in mind that many times the small, cavelike charge serves as God's anteroom leading to the "big city church." Training prepares the preacher for the big city situation.

Another thing these young theologians must be mindful of is the fact that God has chosen some of them to serve permanently in small situations. God alone deserves and reserves the divine right to make some of his ministers a "big fish" in a "small pond." Full many a time I've gone to small towns throughout this country to preach and lecture, and people have pointed preachers out to me and told me that they were the "kingpins" of that town.

God alone can and does make his ministers a "big fish in a small pond." Those ministers are doing a marvelous work for the Lord. And God is richly blessing their labor—crowning it with great success. The Lord of the vineyard will continue to abundantly bless these ministers wherever they are serving in their small situations. And when the "Day of Refreshment" shall have come, he has prepared for them a place in the "house" of his own abode. Thank God for those faithful ministers who are willing to serve wherever the Lord leads them until the final "well done."

Moses did a marvelous job as a shepherd of his father-in-law's flock. Moses married the daughter of Jethro, the priest of Midian, who hired Moses to attend his sheep. Moses did a commendable job. It would do young ministers well to note that as Moses worked his way through his ministerial training, he did not shrink from his job.

Some ministerial students feel like they have a divine right to "get over" on the man as they work their way through colleges and seminaries. But the Lord of the vineyard demands that even ministers of the gospel of Jesus Christ must be faithful over a "few things."

My old seminary dean taught me an unforgettable lesson one day as I observed an indifferent young ministerial student who was doing a halfhearted task cleaning the men's rest room. The dean finally stopped the student and in a fatherly tone told him, "Young man, put your heart and mind to the task here at hand. If you can't do a good job here in this small rest room, how can you succeed at a big church?"

After twenty years, I still remember those words that were spoken by the dean in a small rest room in the men's dorm at my seminary. I worked very hard that day and had my side of that small rest room shining by "knock-off time." I made it my business and my pleasure to keep my side of that small rest room shining each day. Today, after twenty years, my work out on the field is still shining for God!

Young ministers ought to shine daily for God in college and seminary grants, if they expect to shine for him out on the field after training days are over. Jesus called some young men who were shining by the seashore to be his disciples, and how they did shine for the Savior here in this world after he'd ascended into heaven. Today they are shining with him above. We are reminded in the lines of a grand old hymn written by Thomas Shepperd in 1693:

How happy are the saints above,
Who once went sorrowing here!
But now they taste unmingled love,
And joy without a tear.

After Moses had done a marvelous job of leading his flock into grazing grass and water brooks flowing, he led them to Mount Horeb's backside. Here he bumped into God. Preachers ought to strive mightily to be faithful while serving in small situations. For oftentimes, it is while serving faithfully in small situations we bump into God.

Moses bumped into God while serving in a small situation. He was leading sheep on the backside of a mountain when he saw a strange sight. The sight became his magic of the moment. The sight became the maker of his day. He said to himself, "I will now turn aside, and see this great sight, why the bush is not burnt" (Ex. 3:3).

Moses saw the bush, and God saw Moses. And when the Lord saw that he turned aside to see, God called unto him out of the bush, and said, "Moses, Moses. And he said, Here am I" (Ex. 3:4b). The answer of Moses displays the meekness of the man. God loves and uses men of meekness. He uses meek men to topple the power of potentates.

God had respect for the meekness of Moses. He spoke softly and tenderly to Moses, saying, "Draw not nigh hither: put off thy shoes from off thy feet, for the place whereon thou standest is holy ground" (Ex. 3:5).

Many have erred exceedingly by refusing to respect the place whereon they stood in the church of God as holy ground. Let it be known wherever you labor in the Master's vineyard, whatever your task, be it small or great, the place whereon you stand is holy ground. This kingdom-of-heaven-seeking business is indeed holy business. Whether you are a pastor or a policeman or a deacon or a doorkeeper, the place whereon you stand is holy ground.

Let the saints of the living God shout it out to the whole wide world, saying, "The place whereon we stand is holy ground!"

After Moses had obediently put off his shoes, the Lord continued to converse with him:

> Moreover he said, I am the God of Abraham, the God of Isaac, and the God of Jacob. . . . I have surely seen the affliction of my people which are in Egypt, and have heard their cry by reason of their taskmasters; for I know their sorrows; and I am come down to deliver them out of the land of the Egyptians, and to bring them up out of that land into a good land and a large, unto a land flowing with milk and honey; unto the place of the Canaanites, and the Hittites, and the Amorites, and the Perizzites, and the Hivites, and the Jebusites (Ex. 3:6-8).

Standing in awe at the burning bush, Moses admitted his sinking feeling of incompetency. After God had spelled out his divine purpose for his people, Moses let his feeling of inadequacy be known to God. "Who am I, that I should go unto Pharaoh, and that I should bring forth the children of Israel out of Egypt?" (Ex. 3:11).

But God assured Moses of his providential care. No prophet has ever stood before a potentate without the providential protection of God. Nor would Moses. God promised to be with the prophet. He has promised to be with all of his prophets, even unto the end of the world. Prophets need not fear to stand before potentates to tell them what saith the Lord of hosts. Nor should prophets fear being tongue-tied. The power of the Lord of hosts will enable prophets to speak.

God even gave Moses a sign that a divine presence would be with him. And he said, "Certainly I will be with thee; and this shall be a token unto thee, that I have sent thee: When thou hast brought forth the people out of Egypt, ye shall serve God upon this mountain" (Ex. 3:12).

After his sign, Moses wanted to know what name God went by. He requested that God reveal his name in the event the people whom he'd deliver asked it of him. God granted the prophet his request. "And God said unto Moses, I AM THAT I AM: and he said, Thus shalt thou say unto the children of Israel, I AM hath sent me unto you" (Ex. 3:14).

From the burning bush, the prophet went to stand before a potentate. The mighty miracles wrought by God at the burning bush convinced the prophet of providential care. Moses went from the bush to a palace standing on the promises of God.

He had spent forty years in Egypt as a prince. He'd spent forty more years as a shepherd of sheep. He'd spent eighty years getting ready to go for God. Ministers must get ready. Moses got ready and then got gone.

The fearless prophet stood before a chiding potentate. Moses told Pharaoh "Thus saith the Lord." But the hardhearted Pharaoh wanted to know, "Who is the Lord that I should obey him?" (Ex. 5:2). These were harsh words spoken by a mean king to a meek man of God. Moses was not disturbed, nor did he panic. He kept his divine cool. While the potentate ranted and raved in hot displeasure, the prophet remained cool, calm, and confident.

Prophets have a heavenly calmness whenever they stand before potentates. The Lord has willed it so. The prophets Elijah, Daniel, and Jeremiah remained cool, calm, and confident as they stood before potentates.

Moses knew the blessed peace of the nearness of his Lord. He stood before the Pharaoh in the cool confidence of the power of God and told God's message to him. The king would not hear the prophet, so the wrath of the Almighty was poured out in plagues upon the Egyptians. The last plague was the riding of the death angel at midnight. The firstborn of Pharaoh's people died at midnight. The difference being the prophet's people lived because they had the blood. And when the death angel saw the blood, he passed over the house. Happy is that house which has the rich, red, royal blood of Jesus therein. His blood makes the difference.

The prophet triumphed over the potentate. God delivered the children of Israel with a mighty outstretched hand. Moses led them out of Egypt as he was led by the God of the fiery cloud. The reason the Book of Exodus is called the book of grace is that we see the God of glory come down to live with his people. God alone led them and kept them "as the apple of his eye" (Deut. 32:10b).

At the Red Sea, the people griped; the prophet prayed. Here's a lesson to be learned by pastors everywhere. While your congregation protests, you pray. Prayer puts marching into inactive feet. Prayer puts singing upon closed lips. And prayer puts praise upon an acid tongue. Preachers, while people are griping and grumbling, you bend your knees in prayer.

Moses prayed, and God answered. "Speak unto the children of Israel, that they go forward" (Ex. 14:15). Moses marched them across dry-shod. A praying prophet got the job done. The people of God crossed over and looked back from whence they'd come. They saw the chariots and horsemen of Pharaoh no more. A joyful prophet then led the congregation in a victory song:

> Then sang Moses and the children of Israel this song unto the Lord, and spake, saying, I will sing unto the Lord, for he hath triumphed gloriously: the horse and his rider hath he thrown into the sea. The Lord is my strength and song, and he is become my salvation: he is my God, and I will prepare him an habitation; my father's God, and I will exalt him. The Lord is a man of war: the Lord is his name (Ex. 15:1-3).

Moses led the people on—himself being led by the Most High. Their journey was not that far. It was not a long, long way to the Promised Land. When worldliness enters into any congregation, it goes around in circles. Sin slows any people down. Sin walks people around in circles. Sin is a sort of insanity. Sin moves people clockwise. Sin is not a straight-ahead situation. Sin is an around-in-circle situation.

The children of Israel went around in circles for forty years. Moses did not panic. He was a patient prophet. All preachers, especially pastors, would do well to remember that the Master of the vineyard has said, "In your patience possess ye your soul" (Luke 21:19).

Moses was meek, kind, tenderhearted, sweet, and patient. He was a pastor of the rarest kind. On the mountaintop, he received the law which was written by the fingers of God. He had several mountaintop experiences with God. He was vexed by the sins of the people after he'd come down from the holy mount and broke the tablets of stone on which the law had been written. He had to go back to that holy mountain and this time listen to the voice of God and write what God said.

Again, Moses went to the holy mountain. In the eyes of the congregation when it was time for his beloved brother Aaron to depart this earthly life, Moses stripped Aaron of the priestly garments and put them on Eleazar, the son of Aaron. On still another occasion, Moses went to the mountaintop and asked God to show him his face. God explained to Moses that no man could look upon the face of God and live. God hid the prophet in the cleft of the mountain and passed by so that Moses could see his glory.

Patience was a fine point of this great prophet. Even the most patient of prophets are subject to be worn down by the constant impatience of their people. One day the grand old prophet's patience reached the breaking point because of the impatience of his people. He smote the rock and referred to God's people as rebels. He was ordered by God to go to Mount Nebo. This was to be the prophet's last mountaintop experience with God during his earthly life. He'd done his job well, and now it was time for him to bid farewell to the problems of this world.

And Moses went up from the plains of Moab unto the mountain of Nebo, to the top of Pisgah, that is over against Jericho. The Lord showed him all the land of Ephraim, and Manasseh, and all the land of Judah, unto the utmost sea. Moses stood on that mountaintop and saw the plain of the valley of Jericho, the city of palm trees, unto Zoar. What a wonderful sight he saw! He might have been thinking, at that very moment, about another earlier great sight of a burning bush that would not be consumed.

While meditating on the sights he saw, Moses was given his final edict by God. The edict was: "This is the land which I sware unto Abraham, unto Isaac, and unto Jacob, saying, I will give it unto thy seed: I have caused thee to see it with thine eyes, but thou shalt not go over thither" (Deut. 34:4).

The old prophet died there—still strong, still trusting, still meek, still hoping, and still leaning on the Lord. Moses leaned on the Lord till he died. The big Book says so. Moses was 120 years old when he died: his eyes were not dim, nor his natural forces abated.

"So Moses the servant of the Lord died there in the land of Moab, according to the word of the Lord'' (Deut. 34:5). Moses had lived by the word of the Lord and now died by his word. God attended the prophet's funeral. He buried him and then buried his burial. God

> buried him in a valley in the land of Moab, over against Beth-peor: but no man knoweth of his sepulchre unto this day. . . . And there arose not a prophet since in Israel like unto Moses, whom the Lord knew face to face (Deut. 34:6,10).

The old prophet was gone now. He had heard the groans and gripes of the people for the last time. He was gone! He had preached his last sermon and answered God's last earthly call to him. The man was gone! Where had this prophet gone? We know he was a prophet indeed. We know that he had departed, indeed. But what had become of this our departed, preaching brother who was privileged to preach to people and to a potentate?

For an answer, let's go to yet another mountain. Jesus the Lord of life is the "Star of this show." The big Book calls him the Dayspring from on high. Listen to Matthew's account.

> And after six days Jesus taketh Peter, James, and John his brother, and bringeth them up into an high mountain apart, And was transfigured before them: and his face did shine as the sun, and his raiment was white as the light, And, behold, there appeared unto them Moses and Elias talking with him (Matt. 17:1-3).

The answer is given in Matthew's account here. Peter got so carried away when he saw and recognized Moses and Elias talking with Jesus that he thought he'd better do some talking. So Peter cried out: "Lord, it is good for us to be here: if thou wilt, let us make here three tabernacles; one for thee, and one for Moses, and one for Elias" (Matt. 17:4).

Moses, the man of God, stood with the Lord Jesus on the mountaintop. Moses talked with Jesus about the death he should die on Mount Calvary. Moses reminded the Son of God that he had one of two alternatives. He could go back to glory with Moses and Elias, who stood on either side to welcome the Son back to the Father. Or Christ could go on to Calvary and pay the debt of sin that I owed. Jesus dismissed Moses and Elias. The two prophets representing the law and the prophets walked back up those golden stairs forever to be with God the Father who'd spoken out of the cloud, saying, "This is my beloved Son, in whom I am well pleased; hear ye him" (Matt. 17:5*b*). Like Moses who went back home to heaven because he heard the voice of Jesus, I too, heard him say to me, "And as ye go, preach, saying, The kingdom of heaven is at hand" (Matt. 10:7). Like Moses, the meek man of God, I'm on my way back home.

When I Can Read My Title Clear

When I can read my title clear
To mansions in the skies,
I'll bid farewell to ev'ry fear
And wipe my weeping eyes.

Should earth against my soul engage,
And fiery darts be hurled,
Then I can smile at Satan's rage
And face a frowning world.

Let cares, like a wild deluge come,
And storms of sorrow fall!
May I but safely reach my home,
My God, my heav'n, my all.

There shall I bathe my weary soul
In seas of heav'nly rest,
And not a wave of trouble roll
Across my peaceful breast.

Isaac Watts